What people are

Demarcation and I

In *Demarcation and Demystification*, J. Moufawad-Paul advances a militant approach to philosophy against (at least) two contending schools of thought. Against some Marxist interpretations of Marx's famous 11th thesis—those sweeping accusations that philosophy *tout court* is idealist—he defends philosophy as a practice of clarity. And against those new materialists who have mistaken their construction of speculative metaphysics, "new" ontologies, and idiosyncratic objects as synonymous with—or even more important than—transforming the world, he defends a philosophical method grounded in historical materialism and engaged in social struggle. Read this book; it's a manifesto for philosophy.
Devin Zane Shaw, author of *Egalitarian Moments: From Descartes to Rancière*

J. Moufawad-Paul's wide-ranging intervention is a timely and fresh return to the 11th thesis. It forces philosophers to recognize the extent to which their historically recurrent pretension to rise above politics has produced propaganda for the status quo in general, and now liberal propaganda in particular. Deftly unpacking why seemingly radical currents in contemporary ontology actually amount to an occulting, reactionary retreat, the book returns to basics as a means of developing struggle. Whether or not one practices or wishes to practice philosophy in the Maoist terrain, *Demarcation and Demystification* is a major statement on the gulf between what philosophers actually do, and what they think they do.
Matthew R. McLennan, author of *Philosophy and Vulnerability* and *Philosophy, Sophistry, Antiphilosophy*

In this stimulating book, Moufawad-Paul makes a good case that a philosophy of Marxism, a radical practice of interpretation, clarification, and demarcation, is the only way that philosophy can continue in line with the meaning of philosophy after Marx's celebrated 11th thesis. He also confronts head-on the problem of thinking through the relationship between concrete practice, theory, and philosophy and offers a valuable account of the pitfalls of conflating each of these in our work as scientists, theorists, and philosophers. From the standpoint of the critique of bourgeois philosophy, Moufawad-Paul's book is a valuable contribution to our understanding of the meaning of philosophical practice and its place in social transformation.

Mateo Andante, founder of *The Bourgeois Philosophy Project* and Twitter's *@logicians*.

Demarcation and Demystification

Philosophy and its Limits

Demarcation and Demystification

Philosophy and its Limits

J. Moufawad-Paul

Winchester, UK
Washington, USA

JOHN HUNT PUBLISHING

First published by Zero Books, 2019
Zero Books is an imprint of John Hunt Publishing Ltd., No. 3 East St., Alresford,
Hampshire SO24 9EE, UK
office@jhpbooks.com
www.johnhuntpublishing.com
www.zero-books.net

For distributor details and how to order please visit the 'Ordering' section on our website.

Text copyright: J. Moufawad-Paul 2018

ISBN: 978 1 78904 226 9
978 1 78904 227 6 (ebook)
Library of Congress Control Number: 2018953733

A CIP catalogue record for this book is available from the British Library.

Design: Stuart Davies

UK: Printed and bound by CPI Group (UK) Ltd, Croydon, CR0 4YY
US: Printed and bound by Thomson-Shore, 7300 West Joy Road, Dexter, MI 48130

We operate a distinctive and ethical publishing philosophy in
all areas of our business, from our global network of authors to
production and worldwide distribution.

Contents

Also by the author and available from Zero Books

Continuity and Rupture: Philosophy in the Maoist Terrain
Methods Devour Themselves: A Conversation (with Benjanun
Sriduangkaew)

For Samiya: born a year after this book was begun, turning six the year it was completed and submitted. Developing alongside your early life, in the hours when you slept nearby, this project is irrevocably tied to your presence. Hopefully one day these pages will enrich your life as they have been enriched, as have I, by yours.

Author's Note

One question that guides the following pages is, should all philosophical reflections be immediately connected to practice? The answer must be that this would impose too narrow a limit on what is possible to think. [...] Such narrow views about what can be thought should be rejected. Gramsci himself did: socialism is to be developed as a new form of civilization, not just a form of class rule. Furthermore, we can never know what sorts of questions, what sorts of research or philosophical reflections, will prove useful in the long run.
Esteve Morera, Gramsci, Materialism, and Philosophy

For those faithful readers, fellow organizers, and long-time supporters who are familiar with my previously published work, this book might come as a surprise. Unlike *The Communist Necessity* it is not a polemic, nor is it a militant defence of a revolutionary tendency as was the case with *Continuity and Rupture*; it is also not a sequence of theses on a political problematic, a stylistic device I used for *Austerity Apparatus*. What tied these previous works together was an appreciation of the concrete situation, whether general or particular, determined by a desire to propagate communist praxis. *Demarcation and Demystification* might not at first appear to be akin to these other works since it ostensibly concerns philosophy, speaks in the language of philosophy, and is thus somewhat abstract. It does, however, begin where *Methods Devour Themselves*, the book I co-authored with Benjanun Sriduangkaew, left off: with an extended analogy from one of Sriduangkaew's short stories.

This book was begun alongside *Continuity and Rupture*, before even *The Communist Necessity* was conceived, and in fact contributed to some of the conceptual terms that were used in the defence of the Maoist theoretical terrain—including the very term "theoretical terrain". (The claims about what it meant to do philosophy in the terrain of Maoism, the basis of that book, were overdetermined by an earlier draft of the following pages.) Initially my intention was to explain my practice, and what made it different from political economy or social theory, not just to others but to myself as well; I was unaware, in the early stages, of the direction in which it would develop.

Some readers might judge this book as less political than my previous publications because it seems at first glance to be a retreat from the concrete: rather than discussing the meaning of Maoism, the necessity of communism, or the ideology of the current state of affairs, I am instead engaging with abstract questions about the meaning of philosophy and its relationship to Marxism, what it means to practise philosophy as a Marxist, and all of the problematics produced by such a practice. A possible complaint might be that I have descended too far into abstractions. That is, by explaining the philosophical practice that is behind my engagement with the critique I am not contributing to a concrete political practice. In some ways such an assessment is fair: *Demarcation and Demystification* is not as explicitly political as my previous work and, in all honesty, might have more in common with academic Marxism than some of my readers would prefer. I apologize in advance for whatever difficulties I have created for the militants and organizers whose struggles are far more significant and theoretically meaningful than the controversies that conspire in the halls of academia. But bear with me: in order to establish the basis of a revolutionary mass philosophy—a proletarian philosophy—it is necessary to engage with the edifice of academic philosophy, especially that part of this edifice that claims to be on our side.

While I am not disdainful of the preference for non-academic Marxist literature (I understand that a lot of academic Marxism can be annoying), I was trained as an academic and see no reason to uphold the kind of anti-intellectualism that some well-meaning colleagues, similarly trained in universities and colleges, adopt despite their academic background. The fact remains that, rightly or wrongly, my work to date has been driven by a particular philosophical practice, a way of understanding the philosophy of Marxism that has lurked beneath my writing for a while. Moreover, and as I have long maintained, we need to divest ourselves of a particular anti-intellectual bias that is a distortion of an otherwise correct focus on accessibility and mass culture.

Hence, for those who are interested, this book is both an attempt to lay bare the way I approach theoretical problematics and an argument for why other radical philosophers, if they are truly interested in revolutionary transformation, should approach reality in a similar manner. "Philosophy, which once seemed obsolete," Adorno claimed, "lives on because the moment to realize it was missed."[1] Although I do not agree with how Adorno ultimately conceives of philosophical practice, I find this opening remark of *Negative Dialectics* worth reflecting upon. Philosophy is often declared obsolete by both the ideologues of capitalism and the would-be ideologues of a rebel communism. The latter, at least according to Adorno, missed the moment of its realization because they failed to bring into being the transformation that would render philosophical interpretation unnecessary. Since Marx claimed in his eleventh thesis on Feuerbach that philosophers only interpreted the world but the point was to change it, the absence of a change that has succeeded in doing away with capitalism means that, according to Adorno, the moment of interpretation persists because it was never realized in the moment of change and given a meaning beyond interpretation. Despite my disagreement with the definition of philosophy implied by this mobilization of the eleventh thesis, I believe it expresses a partial truth if we alter his statement: "Philosophy, which still seems obsolete, persists once we realize the meaning of its moment." And what do I mean by this? Read on if you find it even slightly intriguing.

What follows should thus be treated as the philosophical scaffolding behind my other books, concretized by the time of *Austerity Apparatus* and inspiring the analogical project of *Methods Devour Themselves*. The scaffolding must necessarily disappear when it comes to works dedicated to political intervention, true, but at the same time it is worth investigating the basis for such scaffolding and why it exists in the first place. This book thus represents the philosophical staging of everything I have produced to date. The following pages function as a small clearing ground of Western "radical" philosophy in the interest of operationalizing a philosophical practice that, while engaging with the most radical aspects of metropolitan philosophy, can be placed in the service of revolutionary theory. Such a practice will hopefully promote an opening for marginalized counter-narratives that are truly universal.

Engaging philosophy as an object of thought runs the risk of becoming obscurantist regardless of one's intentions due to the rarified language of philosophical discourse. While I have tried my best to be clear and refuse the temptation to obfuscate I realize that this might not always be possible. Unless one is a very good writer, because it takes a considerable amount of skill to make difficult concepts easy to grasp, clarity (which should be the goal of philosophy) is often elusive. At the very least I hope to have provided others interested in thinking through philosophy from a Marxist position with a sort of "what is philosophy?" text for radicals. Not that this book is another "what is philosophy?" book because it is only partially interested in this question, but it is fair to deem it a mini-manual for would-be philosophers interested in a militant commitment to anti-capitalism.

In the life and death struggle of socialism against barbarism, where the possibility of the latter's victory is becoming more visceral with each year, philosophers also must contribute their skills to a mass movement against the present state of affairs. We must become militants dedicated to the communist necessity rather than imagine that we sit on the sidelines, above and beyond class struggle. We owe it to ourselves, others, and philosophy itself to get our hands dirty, practise philosophy within a mass movement, and help bring about the denouement of emancipation.

Notes

1. Adorno, *Negative Dialectics*, 3.

When the reality is described, a self-sufficient philosophy loses its medium of existence. At the best its place can only be taken by a summing-up of the most general results, abstractions which are derived from the observation of the historical development of men. These abstractions in themselves, divorced from real history, have no value whatsoever. They can only serve to facilitate the arrangement of historical material, to indicate the sequence of its separate strata. But they by no means afford a recipe or schema, as does philosophy, for neatly trimming the epochs of history.
Karl Marx and Friedrich Engels

In the battle that is philosophy all the techniques of war, including looting and camouflage, are permissible.
Louis Althusser

Prologue

philosophy and radical practice

In Benjanun Sriduangkaew's story *Comet's Call*, an alien civilization is subjected to the ravages of a "denouement machine", a slow and terrible weapon that is "aimed at certain lines of ancestry".[1] The product of an insurrection led by the cultural nationalists of an oppressed minority, the machine has devastated large swathes of the population while simultaneously failing to secure its engineer's insurrectionary aims. When the machine was triggered, one of the story's characters explains, "A few onlookers unraveled instantly; as a distant offshoot, I decay at a more sedate pace. But the conclusion is the same, equally inevitable." All attempts to understand the meaning of the machine, the conceptual terrain in which it operates, according to its own logic, are stymied: "The exact nature of its mechanism eludes all," explains another character, "our engineers may not approach it and monitoring devices malfunction in proximity." The terrain upon which the machine acts is determined by a logic of ethnicity that has generated the truth procedure of a race war; its civilizational geography is such that its subjects are tied to its logic. The terrain of the city-state has thus become "a sealed sphere: except at entry points and exits—and each allows only one or the other—none may enter or leave". Upon this terrain the denouement machine acts by drawing violent lines of demarcation, forcing its meaning to become clear. Although the machine's tracing of ancestral lines, following the rules of the terrain's race logic, results in annihilation, this is simply an act of revealing the truth claims upon which the civilization depended: racial purity is a myth and, once this logic is revealed by the machine, the terrain cannot survive its own logic.

What is interesting in this fantastic story is that all attempts to make sense of the machine according to the logic of the terrain upon which it operates result in failure. Enter the character Ziyi, a near mythic outsider, who is hired to understand and arrest the machine. In order to solve the machine's riddle she is forced to act in tandem with its function by disposing of its primary targets—the decadent upper caste rulers most threatened by the insurrection's machine—and thus accomplishes the machine's aim. Moreover, Ziyi is not a passive observer. Despite being sheltered from the machine's ravages she knows people in this civilization; her solution requires her to also make a political choice and her interaction with the machine cannot be separated from this choice.

What Sriduangkaew's story illustrates is the practice of philosophy that will be explored in this book. Firstly, like the fictional civilization, there are terrains that possess their own logic, truth procedures, and contours of meaning. Secondly, like the denouement machine, there is the operation of philosophy that attempts to excavate the logic of these pre-existing terrains, forcing meaning through demarcation and sharpening clarity. Philosophy is thus like a denouement because it seeks to draw all the strands of the narrative it engages together even if sometimes, like in this story, it might result in the kind of intervention intended to undermine the stability of its object of critique. Thirdly, like Ziyi, there is the philosopher whose intervention, which necessarily forces demarcation by the very fact that it is declaring meaning (which will simultaneously mean it is declaring the opposite, non-meaning), is never truly exterior, practising from an abstractly pure archimedian point, but will always remain troubled by various choices generated by their social position in relation to the theoretical terrain.

To simplify what might read at this point as needlessly arcane: truth claims regarding existence are generated by theory, this theory is a terrain in that the truth claims it makes often develop according to their own procedural logic, philosophy's task is to clarify and demarcate the terrain of theory so as to force meaning, and philosophers are always compromised (even if they think otherwise) by political commitments. A scientist establishes through the concrete practice of their discipline a theory that speaks in the name of *fact* and *truth*; this theory as it is developed and explored by its progenitors and others develops successive truths; philosophy attempts to investigate and explain what these truths mean for our lived existence, the philosophers involved in this investigation are already dedicated to certain other truths about existence.

Comet's Call thus describes what I take to be the practice of philosophy: an intervention upon the terrain of theory so as to force meaning. At first this intervention appears outside of the terrain, unconditioned by its logic, and indeed must be practised exogenously—just as a cartographer embedded in a given landscape charts their map from an imaginary bird's eye perspective. But our understanding of philosophical practice following the materialist break signalled by Marx and Engels must also recognize the imaginary dimension of this exterior: philosophy, despite the beliefs of many philosophers, does not emerge from a social void. The character of Ziyi who other characters believe to be "not human but a comet that has chosen anthropoid form" is a good metaphor of this mythic outside philosopher—imagined to be outside of business as usual, like a comet that intervenes from the void of space—suddenly pulled down into the messy world of social relations, profaned by the materialist injunction that recognizes the inability of philosophy to ever escape social and historical relations. "Revolutionaries and their dreadful bargains," Ziyi complains when she is forced to realize that she must choose a side in a terrain that she imagined herself above, "zealots and their terrible ideals". But she still collaborates with these social relations which are also the solution to the riddle she was hired to solve; the meaning discovered is determined by the operations of the denouement machine.

But we are getting ahead of ourselves. Before we can even explain, argue for, and declare the above definition of philosophy—that it is an intervention upon a theoretical terrain and is never purely sequestered from this terrain or another—there are a number of prior problematics we need to explore. The most obvious problem, here, is whether we are justified in defining the practice of philosophy, specifically philosophy that takes its cue from Marxism, in such a way. This problem, which is a necessary starting point, will be the focus of the first chapter. Such a starting point, however, requires a prologue that asks the following question: why bother with a definition of philosophy in the first place?

Defining philosophy

Defining *philosophy* has always been a philosophical conceit. Philosophers often treat their discipline as an object of study and are perhaps too obsessed with such an inward turning investigation. While part of this obsession is in part due to a common confusion over the meaning of philosophy evinced by new university students and laypersons who assume, based on a common sense understanding, that to practise philosophy is simply to express one's personal beliefs and opinions about existence, it is also a fact that treating philosophy itself as an object of study is a tendency that arises from the discipline's most basic logic: to locate a terrain of study and attempt to force meaning. As Wittgenstein wrote in the *Tractatus*, "philosophy aims at the logical clarification of thoughts",[2] and so it is understandable that philosophers would also attempt to clarify their thoughts on the meaning of philosophy itself. Hence, we should not be surprised when we encounter entire libraries of books written by famous philosophers devoted to providing a definition of their discipline.

If the task of finding a definition of philosophy in general

has resulted in an avalanche of scholarship, the task of finding a
definition of philosophy in the shadow of Marx's eleventh thesis
on Feuerbach—where we are told that philosophy has interpreted
the world but the point is to change it—has produced its own
difficulties and debates. Regardless of one's particular thoughts
on Marx's project, the influence of Marxism upon philosophy
as a whole is undeniable; it has indeed cast a shadow across the
entire field. Although Marx's influence is particularly significant
in the realm of social philosophy, even amongst those radical
theorists who begin by rejecting its "totalizing narrative", it has
also provoked the engagement of epistemologists, logicians, and
philosophers of science. Moreover, those philosophers utterly
opposed to all forms of Marxist politics often become invested
in dismissing Marx and Marxism (i.e. Karl Popper went to some
length to argue that it was a "cargo-cult") falling over themselves
to cleanse the respectable field of political philosophy from the
shadow of Marxism.

While some might argue that, with the collapse of actually
existing socialism and capitalism's so-called "end of history",
Marxism's influence is no longer significant, this fails to
recognize that the line Marx drew through philosophy, the
scission of *interpretation* and *transformation*, may in fact be
as salient and undeniable as earlier lines drawn by the first
philosophers, by heretical theorists such as Ibn Khaldun, or by
the new scientists of the European Enlightenment. There are
moments when philosophical practice was transformed and I
will argue that the emergence of Marxism represents its most
apocalyptic transformation.

Simply assuming that Marxism has been influential, and that
the questions it posed for philosophy remain significant, does
little to answer the more important question: what is the meaning
of the shadow it casts upon the entirety of philosophical practice,
if it indeed casts such a shadow, and how can we understand the
meaning of philosophy, both Marxist and non-Marxist, within

its twilight? If understanding the meaning of philosophy in general has been a problem for the entire history of philosophy, figuring out the meaning of its Marxist instantiation is similarly troublesome since Marxists also cannot decide on a definition of "Marxist philosophy". Indeed, the history of Marxism—from its most orthodox to its most heterodox variants—is filled with statements regarding philosophy and its relationship to Marxism. As we shall examine, some of these statements have been quite formulaic whereas others have been rather vague.

This book, then, exists as an attempt to make sense of the meaning of philosophy in general through the lens of the meaning of Marxist philosophy in particular. The former concern is guided by the latter since we cannot escape the fact that our general definitions are mediated by our political fidelity; even this claim is essentially "Marxist", one that will most probably be rejected by other philosophers whose commitments are at odds with the politics of this book. In any case, political commitment aside, this book will not be a typical "what is philosophy?" (or even a "what is Marxist philosophy?") treatise. Rather, this project is guided by two questions: i) what is philosophy's relationship to radical theory and practice?; ii) what does it mean to radically practise philosophy? My aim is not merely to define philosophy in general, and Marxist philosophy in particular, but to do so in a manner that clarifies a radical intervention upon social theory and revolutionary practice. Philosophy, therefore, in the shadow of the eleventh thesis.

Drawing lines of demarcation is useful for both thinking and for what Louis Althusser called "theoretical-practice"; I am not primarily concerned with teaching laypersons about what philosophers do, or even clarifying my chosen disciplinary field for others within this field, since this would result in an introductory or beginners' book that would have no practical application beyond disciplinary definition. Instead, by proposing a scission between philosophy and theory, and thus putting philosophy in its place, the aim is to force questions about what it means to engage with social theory and radical praxis. How, then, should we understand a multiplicity of social theories, as well as the historical unfolding of critical thought, in relationship to innumerable rebellions and radical rejections of oppression, exploitation, normative discourses, and ideological hegemony? Those of us who are interested in making sense of any and all phenomena according to a radical theoretical-practice often find ourselves dizzied by myriad and contradictory social theories. The temptation is to cherry-pick from disparate theoretical constellations in the hope that radical eclecticism will force meaning. Hence, a radical theoretical-practice may indeed require clarity.

Moreover, I am also interested in producing such clarity by forcing a confrontation between radical social theory and revolutionary practice. The gap between academic theory and revolutionary theory, and the fact that many enamoured by the former might be unaware of the latter (and vice versa), is a dissonant space that needs to be bridged. Contemporary social theory may teach us something about revolutionary movements, but these movements should also teach us something about social theory and how theory relates to all types of social practice— from revolutionary practice itself, to social struggles, to all forms of human production and creation, to even intellectual and artistic critique. An understanding of this gap will deepen our understanding of theory and practice, as well as theoretical-practice, and thus spills beyond a mere definition of philosophy.

Therefore, while I believe in the importance of social theory, I also do not hold that academic study should be treated as identical to revolutionary politics. Rather, I would argue that the best works of social theory (as well as scientific, artistic and literary praxis) emerge from sites of struggle and what some Marxists call "a concrete analysis of a concrete situation". That is, engagement with actual revolutionary practice and concrete instances of class struggle (broadly understood) produces better radical theory as well as better radical theorists, political economists, historians, scientists, artists, and especially philosophers.

Some caveats

Since, as indicated above, this is not intended to be a typical "what is philosophy?" book, though it will have to deal with this question, I want to be clear that the ways in which I define philosophy and philosophical praxis, limited as they are to very specific problematics, will necessarily differ from many other books focused solely on this question—either for specialists or non-specialists. Hence, the metaphorical language I will be using (much of which crept into my conceptual tool-kit before and during the long process of this manuscript's development[3]) to describe philosophy is not meant to possess any sense of theoretical universality. As I will argue: i) it might make sense to draw a conceptual distinction between *theory* and *philosophy*; ii) I am not doing ontology in the grand sense of the word and creating, to reference Feuerbach's critique of Hegel, a "speculative theology".

Rather, the following pages are a series of reflections regarding philosophy's function in relation to social practice. I will demarcate my approach from others, and hopefully provide some compelling arguments as to why such a demarcation is important. Although I will put forward certain conceptual terms (i.e. theoretical terrain, clarity, occultation, annihilation, spontaneity, catastrophe) that I find useful in explaining my approach, these terms are not meant to be the final word on the subject; they are intended for semantic precision and I thus have no problem if they are rejected by the reader in favour of terms that are more precise. My project is driven by an ethos that is opposed to philosophical codification; it is intended to force an appreciation of the sequence of theoretical truth generation existing before and outside of the practice of philosophy as the only thing that can establish tendencies, schools, and militant fidelities.

Furthermore, although I will define philosophy as an endeavour that interprets rather than changes the world, while indicating the radical importance of the former, I am definitely not arguing that a refusal to engage in projects of political transformation is philosophically meaningful. The radical practice of interpretation (which, as we shall discuss, includes clarification and demarcation) is only possible if the philosopher is engaged in concrete political praxis. As a militant the philosopher's work is borne from and contributes to the struggle for a better world. Philosophy does not change the world but it can provide the tools capable of clarifying world-changing movements that, as we shall examine, operate outside of the philosophical ambit.

This book does not aim to be a political manifesto, or any attempt to establish an order of the political real—a revolutionary programme, a doctrine that by itself seeks radical change—because this should not be, as I will argue in the following chapters, the role of philosophy. Manifestos are produced by actual revolutionary movements (whether they be grand and earth-shaking social movements or small but important artistic/literary/film movements); political programmes are produced by revolutionary organizations that have concretely investigated their circumstances and are part of that mass motion from which radical social theory can properly emerge. Philosophy needs to take these circumstances as an object of thought; philosophers need to recognize that we are not the initiators but, like the character Ziyi in Sriduangkaew's story, agents that at first appear to drop from the sky only to discover that their interventions are bound up in all the messiness of the truth procedures of multiple theoretical terrains.

Notes

1. This story was originally published in the August 2016 issue of *Mythic Delirium* (http://mythicdelirium.com/featured-story-%E2%80%A2-august-2016). Since my previous book, *Methods Devour Themselves*, was co-authored with Sriduangkaew it is perhaps appropriate that I begin this treatise with an "analogical assemblage" culled from her work. To be clear, however, this prologue was written before *Methods Devour Themselves* was conceived as a project.

2. Wittgenstein, §4.112.

3. For example, the concept of the "theoretical terrain" is a concept that I developed in an early draft of this manuscript while also working on *Continuity and Rupture* and thus found its way into that book.

Chapter One

philosophy and the eleventh thesis

The philosopher is a worker in another sense: detecting, presenting and associating the truths of his or her time, reviving those that have been forgotten and denouncing inert opinion, s/he is the welder of separate worlds.
Alain Badiou, Second Manifesto for Philosophy

In the eighteenth century, Immanuel Kant, enamoured with the European Enlightenment, proclaimed his intention to pursue a Copernican Revolution in philosophy. Recognizing the significance of the rise of the new sciences, those emergent and coherent theoretical terrains from which numerous truths were being explored, and worrying about Hume's problem of induction (that implied there was no logical-philosophical basis for these scientific endeavours), Kant wanted to place metaphysics on an equal footing with the sciences. His assumption was that the sciences required the firm foundation of philosophy; that all pursuits of knowledge must, in order to properly count as knowledge, possess a philosophical basis. Indeed, Hume spurred him to pursue this assumption by demonstrating that causal reasoning might not possess any philosophical basis. Kant thus felt that philosophy needed to catch up to the European Enlightenment. Without philosophical stability, the reasoning goes, all theoretical engagements with existence would be doomed to incoherence.

Such an assumption, however, is as old as so-called "Western" philosophy itself. The belief that philosophy (and particularly metaphysics/ontology) is the "queen" of all knowledge, including science, and that there can be no truth procedure[1] without philosophy is a conceit that is so pervasive it is nearly banal. From Plato onwards attempts to provide grand metaphysical or ontological systems that strengthen reality with philosophical scaffolding have determined the history of the canon. In the early modern period Descartes attempted to refound knowledge on firm philosophical principles, thus bequeathing us with that troublesome notion of the subject, and even analytic philosophy has been concerned with the rules of logico-philosophical first principles. The claim that x theory needs "philosophical grounding" is common in some sectors of sociology; the idea that we do philosophy first so as to structure the operations of theory is the ethos of philosophy's narrative. We can perhaps call this conceit, following François Laruelle, the "philosophical decision"—that is, the a priori and often hidden decision philosophy makes about how to divide and structure our world according to its operations.

The pervasiveness of this conceit, however, has not persisted without challenge. Feuerbach, after becoming exasperated with Hegel, dismissed this grand practice of philosophy as "speculative theology". More recently, Quentin Meillassoux has suggested that the philosophical canon rests on a "correlationist" fallacy that refuses to admit that scientific claims about an existence predating humanity's ability to philosophize counts as proper knowledge.[2] Even still, the preeminence philosophy accords itself regarding knowledge remains an essential part of the discipline, at least in the Western tradition which, because of the history of modern colonialism, has come to determine the meaning and direction of "the canon". If this preeminence is no longer explicitly apparent, it remains a common attitude. All talk about creating or discovering a philosophical basis to this-or-that theoretical approach is evidence of this attitude's persistence.

There was a historical moment where the above problem was temporarily decentred, or at the very least shaken to its core, and this moment was the event of Marxism. This decentring, however, was one of confusion. For in its attempt to produce a scientific theory of society/history, Marxism was wagered as a decisive break from political philosophy while at the same time (based on Marx and Engels' relationship to the discipline of philosophy and what they had learned from Hegel and Feuerbach) using philosophy to accomplish this supposed break. The mixture of scientific-social theory and political philosophy resulted in a confusion because Marx and Engels only cursively outlined how they understood philosophy in relation to what they called science. The break from the long-standing philosophical conceit was thus never complete because it lacked a thorough articulation. On the one hand philosophy was put in its place, eventually and particularly by orthodox Marxism-Leninism, and thus treated as separate from but parallel to the rugged practice of historical materialist *science.* On the other hand, philosophy—specifically *Marxist* philosophy—was treated as an unfinished project, something that needed to be completed so as to give historical materialism proper metaphysical foundations. Hence, despite Marxism's attempt to break from philosophy's preeminence, the conceit of the philosophical decision would return within Marxism itself: more than one Marxist philosopher has argued that Marxism ought to return to the business of doing philosophy so as to provide firmer ontological foundations for historical materialism. The historical failure of communism is thus interpreted as partly the result of a philosophical weakness: Marxism's refusal or inability to articulate clear philosophical foundations.

But I want to argue that the strength of Marxism's influence on philosophy lies in its break from this long-standing philosophical conceit. The problem is not a lack of philosophical foundations but that this demand for philosophical foundations is part of the idealism that Marxism sought to dispel in its attempt to invert the way in which the world is understood. Indeed, Sylvain Lazarus conceptualizes Marx's project as a fundamental rupture from philosophy:

> Marx will try to shift the [Hegelian] dialectic from a conception which involves structures of thought to one that requires operators which are themselves historical entities, that is to say, materialist. The central operator is clearly that of class (keep in mind that Lenin will add that of the Party). The break between Marx and Hegel is played out in this debate on the dialectic, and although it is, to be sure, a break from idealism, it is even more a break with philosophy.[3]

Marx's "break" can be conceived according to a simple reversal: philosophical thinking is not foundational but in fact dependent on a process of knowledge production that is not philosophical. At the same time, though, it would be erroneous to presume that Marx was dispensing with philosophy altogether since there was still something "philosophical", but in a weaker and less central sense, to his approach; this *something* is what we will explore. The Marxist "break with philosophy" is a break from its central conceit, that philosophy is the foundation of knowledge—philosophy-qua-philosophy. Instead philosophy and philosophical practice possess a significant role in making sense of the world if they are put in their proper place.

But the reason why the above claim about the Marxist "break with philosophy" is difficult to argue is akin to why Meillassoux finds it difficult to argue against correlationism: the moment you try to prove that something that draws the boundaries of speculative thought is also seeing/thinking the world through a "camera obscura",[4] you cannot help but speak in the terms determined by these boundaries. For example, the moment you claim that philosophy is not foundational is the very moment you can be accused of making a foundational philosophical statement; the well is poisoned, it seems naive to suggest you can escape the philosophical decision because by doing so you are making another decision. But I would like to suggest that this is less a philosophical decision than a decision about philosophy, and in order to begin thinking through these boundaries it is useful to start with the most quoted statement Marx made about philosophy and its role: the eleventh thesis on Feuerbach.

Marx's eleventh thesis

At the conclusion of *Theses on Feuerbach*, Marx states, in the eleventh and final thesis, that "philosophers have only *interpreted* the world in various ways; the point is to *change* it".[5] Thus, those of us who are labouring under the auspices of "Marxist philosophy" are often forced to wonder about the meaningfulness of our work and whether or not philosophy as a discipline possesses any worth. While it could be the case that *Theses on Feuerbach* might not be a useful foundation for a definition of philosophy because they are "no more than a set of rather ambiguous aphorisms"[6] that take up only a page or two, and more importantly are mainly a response to the work of Ludwig Feuerbach, the eleventh thesis, despite what Marx may or may not have intended, is often cited as a definition (if not *the* definition) of the Marxist philosophical project. Instead of simply rejecting this thesis and the essay in which it resides as useless due to historical limitations, then, I believe it is far more fruitful to grant it the importance it has been accorded; it has historically functioned as an axiom for Marxist philosophy.

Hence I will treat the eleventh thesis as an invitation to thought so as to suggest a particular approach to philosophy that is demarcated from the traditional ways in which the thesis is interpreted. That is, even if it is indeed the case that this set of theses that ends with Marx's dictum about changing the world was in fact nothing more than a set of scattered thoughts mainly about delineating Marx's project from Feuerbach's, it is also true that the eleventh thesis rightly or wrongly casts a shadow over the business of Marxist philosophy. This shadow has been lengthened by thinkers such as Georg Lukács, Antonio Gramsci, Theodor Adorno, Louis Althusser and many others. Marxists interested in philosophy thus find themselves working under this shadow and the ways in which it has been defined regardless of its original intention, if this in fact can be known. Historically, amongst the larger Marxist population, the eleventh thesis has been given three general interpretations. I believe that all of these interpretations are simultaneously incorrect and correct definitions of the philosophical project of Marxism, the result of the thesis statement's particular amphibology. My interpretation, however, will read the aphorism of the eleventh thesis in light of the Marxist project as a whole, a project that conceived of itself as a science and that, as I have argued in *Continuity & Rupture*, has developed according to key world historical revolutions. In order to get to my interpretation, though, we should briefly examine the three general interpretations of the eleventh thesis that are most commonly circulated.

First of all, there are those who argue that philosophy as a discipline, unless it is simply the method of "dialectical materialism", is primarily idealist. Doctrinaire Marxism-Leninism, codified in the Soviet textbook division between historical and dialectical materialism, best represents this perspective. The claim, here, is that, outside of the philosophical method of dialectical materialism, true Marxists must engage instead with political economy, the key material science of reality, thus rejecting anything that smacks of philosophy. This interpretation imagines that engagement with political economy is somehow free from philosophical presuppositions, denying that political economists may also only be what Althusser called "spontaneous philosophers" who lack the perspective, due to their impoverished definition of philosophy, to realize that many of their commitments are based on unexamined philosophical decisions.[7] Significantly, though, this interpretation of the eleventh thesis correctly warns against a retreat into the realm of

22

ideas, the spectre of Platonism that threatens, however vaguely, every philosopher.

Secondly, there are those who claim that Marx was only correct insofar as he projected his statement into the future: the point is to change the world but only when this world is properly "interpreted"—Marx simply assumed, too quickly, that the work of philosophical interpretation ended with Hegel. Thus, as Adorno appears to argue in *Negative Dialectics*, in order to provide a proper philosophical basis for changing the world, the realm of change (of praxis, of revolutionary action) must be delayed in order to work out the details of the correct foundational philosophy. Contemporary thinkers such as Slavoj Zizek have evinced this understanding of the eleventh thesis, arguing for a revalorization of the realm of interpretation so as to fix the failed attempts at political change. This interpretation breaks the link between theory and practice, advocating a return to the ivory tower where privileged thinkers will provide a new basis for future revolutionary struggles—what Devin Zane Shaw has termed "a kind of idealist revanchism".[8] At the same time, however, this position warns against the crude anti-intellectualism prevalent amongst some Marxists who would seek to ban all philosophical interpretation because of their assumption that the Marxist tradition has already worked out philosophy and requires no reconsideration

Finally, there are those—such as Henri Lefebvre in *Metaphilosophy*—who read the concluding passage of *Theses on Feuerbach* as meaning the following: "philosophers [until now] have only interpreted the world, the point is [for philosophers or philosophy] to change it". That is, the role of philosophers is to produce revolution rather than interpretation. While this position is correct insofar as it demands that philosophers stake their thought in the realm of political practice, it is also a confusion of theory and practice because it imagines that philosophy by itself—or philosophers by themselves—can somehow produce revolutionary change. I am reminded here of those tiny communist grouplets that mistake the preservation and articulation of a pure ideological position (in their papers and slogans) as somehow identical to political organizing. Despite these problems, this position warns against losing sight of the need for every self-proclaimed Marxist, philosophers included, to focus on the necessity of changing the world.

Propositions regarding interpretation

I would like to suggest a different approach to defining Marx's concluding thesis, one that borrows something from all three of the above positions, that will initiate a productive understanding of philosophy. It is my contention that the eleventh thesis can be used to signify a rupture with the way in which, *hitherto*, philosophy has been understood as a practice. My intention is to open a critique of the way philosophy has historically understood itself while simultaneously suggesting that philosophy has always been, and can only be, something other than its illusions. This approach might not have been Marx's intention when he wrote the eleventh thesis but I think the definition I will suggest is in line with the overall Marxist project. Moreover, it is doubtful that other conceptualizations of the eleventh thesis—all of which begin by assuming a single aphoristic sentence is a materialist axiom—are any more correct. Indeed, I would argue that in light of the larger Marxist project they are in fact *incorrect* and that my interpretation, at the very least, interprets the eleventh thesis in a manner that is congruent with the unfolding dynamic of historical materialism.

In order to understand the role philosophy should play for those who take Marx's project seriously, as well as what philosophy *is*, I would like to suggest five general propositions that will guide the discussion of this entire book:

***Proposition #1:** Philosophy not only *has* interpreted the world but it only ever *can* interpret the world. It does not possess the ability by itself to change anything—people change the world, just as they are changed by it. Nor are the people who change the world small cabals of philosopher-kings; they are the masses, collective subjects in motion.

*Proposition #2: It is somewhat inaccurate to speak of "Marxist philosophy" because philosophy can only be something that interprets—it does not produce ruptures and new universal understandings of reality but attempts to make sense, providing clarity, of what is given. Philosophy is that which takes problems encountered in reality—contradictions, established concepts, ideas, fields of thought—as objects of interpretation and reflection. (It can also, therefore, take itself as its own object of reflection.) So instead of "Marxist philosophy" we should speak of "the philosophy of Marxism".

*Proposition #3: Philosophy, that which can only interpret the world, is not synonymous with theory. Thus a philosophy of politics should not be confused with political theory or political economy, though political economy and political theory may often possess unquestioned philosophical commitments—unexamined interpretative ideologies—just as some political economists and political theorists might mistake their work for philosophy.

*Proposition #4: Since philosophy is that which can only interpret the world, and philosophers do not interpret the world from the void because they are *in* the world, philosophy possesses class commitments.[9] Hence we can speak of bourgeois philosophy (that which interprets the world from a position that begins from a ruling class perspective), proletarian philosophy (that which begins by rejecting the ruling class reality), and multiple confused class positions in between. This is why Alain

Badiou has argued "that every philosophy is conditioned by a *real* politics".[10]

*Proposition #5: Change comes from practice—and a philosophical understanding of Marxism might help to argue for this fact—not from philosophical contemplation. The universal developments of Marxist theory emerge from the successes and failures of world historical revolutions, *not* from philosophy. Within the theoretical terrain of Marxism, philosophy is an interpretive gesture that investigates and engages problems encountered in this terrain.

My argument is that Marx's eleventh thesis should be understood as a statement that is meant to provide clarity about philosophy's role in revolutionary theory and practice. As a thinker who was above all concerned with revolution, Marx did not believe that the practice of philosophy was more important than the practice of revolutionary politics; it makes sense to read the eleventh thesis in this light. While philosophy can possibly reflect upon and make sense of revolutionary theory, it cannot by itself produce the theory necessary for social transformation; such theory emerges from revolutionary movements. The philosopher might be able to provide clarity for this theory but, unless they are engaged in those movements attempting to change the world for the better, their contributions might end up being little more than banal contemplation.

The role of a philosopher of Marxism, therefore, should be nothing more or less than the role of an investigator attempting to make sense of the established conditions of Marxism. Since the conditions of Marxism include political economy and historical materialism, these are also areas that require philosophical investigation. Moreover, the conditions of Marxism are conditions that are both internally and externally contentious: various Marxists argue about what they mean, just as various non- or anti-Marxists argue against their very existence Here, the role of the philosopher of Marxism is to investigate these arguments and attempt to bring clarity to such contradictions and debates.

The philosopher of Marxism must also practice the philosophy of political economy and the philosophy of historical materialism—not to mention the philosophy of revolutionary ethics and the philosophy of the revolutionary subject—while remaining cognizant of the fact that they are working from a position that is already political. To imagine otherwise is to confuse contemplation with social practice. As I stated in the third proposition, philosophers are never outside of the world, never beyond class struggle.

And yet political economists sometimes also, as aforementioned, imagine that they are outside of class and history—even when they call themselves *Marxist*—often confusing their abstractions with reality. This is why you can have two political economists, each with properly "mathematical" and "empirical" data, who produce opposing conclusions. In this situation, the role of the philosopher who decides to involve themselves in such a debate is not to argue on the level of political economy; philosophizing political economy should never be confused with political economy proper, or vice versa, just as philosophizing science should not be confused with science proper. Rather, philosophy can provide a second-order perspective to political economy by investigating whether or not a political economic commitment is rational, historical, and/or ethical by bringing it into contact with the larger concrete circumstances from which it emerged.

Does a supposedly empirical statement about class composition, for example, make sense when judged against the historical fact of the class being described by the political economist? Do the conclusions of a specific political economist produce logical corollaries that are rationally unfeasible? What are the ethical concerns raised by a specific political economy position? These are some of the many questions a philosopher of political economy, rather than a political economist, might ask. They are similar to the sorts of questions a philosopher of science would ask a scientist.

The comparison of the philosophy of political economy to the philosophy of science is salient because the latter's tradition speaks to my concerns regarding philosophical clarity. Since scientists are usually not philosophers, they often do not philosophize about the situation in which their scientific practice is embedded. The scientist practising physiognomy in the nineteenth century was not a bad *scientist* if he did not investigate the ethical questions of his practice (we know now that he was not even a scientist, bad or good), but the philosopher who did not question whether or not physiognomy should even be considered *science*, and who did not raise the second-order questions of ethics and logical veracity, would be a terrible philosopher indeed.

Therefore, philosophy's role in these circumstances is to investigate the terms of the debate, reflect on the boundaries of the discussion, rationally engage with the constraints of the argument and attempt to provide the clarity that will produce deliberation. Or, as Badiou has argued, "philosophy confronts thinking as a choice, thinking as decision. Its proper task is to make the choice clear. Hence, we can say: a philosophical situation involves the moment in which a choice is proclaimed –a choice of existence, or a choice of thinking."[11] Philosophy is an intervention, akin to the intervention made by the character Ziyi in my prologue's analogy, that demarcates and machinates for denouement and resolution.

Marxist philosophy and the philosophy of Marxism

I have chosen to use *the philosophy of Marxism* rather than *Marxist philosophy* because, like many philosophers, I am interested in a particular semantic precision. While these two terms are often used interchangeably, I believe they imply very different definitions of philosophy and the role of the philosopher in relation to the universe of Marxism.

Marxist philosophy, simply put, refers to the methodology that emerges from the science of history established by Marx and Engels: the dialectical materialism that accompanies historical materialism. Louis Althusser, one of the twentieth century's greatest philosophical investigators of Marxist theory, argued that "the birth of a new philosophy is simultaneous with the foundation of a new science, and this science [meaning Marxism] is the science of history".[12]

Philosophers who are also Marxists, even if they accept (as I do) that their philosophical method is dialectical materialism, are not simply applying, mechanically and unreflectively, "diamat" axioms to the problems they choose to investigate. Philosophically investigating the Marxist problematic, even as a Marxist, should never mean the crude and mechanical application of a particular method; the philosopher is always required to reflect on this method, to interpret its meaning at every given moment and conjuncture, rather than assume that its logical victory is eternally secure. In philosophy, to appropriate a phrase from Fanon, the methods should always devour themselves.

After the passage cited above, Althusser would argue further: "as the new philosophy was only implicit in the new science it might be tempted to *confuse itself with it. The German Ideology* sanctions this confusion as it reduces philosophy...to a faint shadow of science, if not to the empty generality of positivism."[13]

By imagining that crudely performing the Marxist philosophical method is synonymous with philosophical investigation, we might as well accept the first interpretation of Marx's eleventh thesis on Feuerbach, discussed above, and have nothing to do with philosophy since, if it is simply reducible to a method, it is less useful than Marxist "science".

29

Moreover, the term *Marxist philosophy* might imply an even more dubious interpretation: the confusion of philosophical investigation with theoretical development. For if the term already confuses philosophy with the science from which it emerged, then it is likely that philosophers might confuse themselves with revolutionary theoreticians and imagine, in defiance of the methodology they claim to espouse, that they are establishing new theoretical principles, that philosophical investigations produced within the sphere of contemplation are somehow as valuable, if not more so, than those theories and theoreticians that have emerged from the crucible of concrete revolutionary practice.

If there is a confusion between the philosophy and science of Marxism then it is very likely (and indeed it has happened more than once!) that philosophers will imagine that the performance of revolutionary philosophy is identical to the performance of revolutionary science and that the "new" concepts they theorize, most often from the void of academic contemplation, are identical to the concepts established by revolutions and revolutionary figures. The second and third aforementioned understandings of Marx's final thesis on Feuerbach demonstrate this confusion. If a philosopher such as Theodor Adorno could advocate a return to philosophical contemplation, and write an entire book arguing for new foundational concepts for revolutionary theory, then it is clear that he imagined himself to be on the same theoretical level as Marx, Engels, Lenin, or Mao. But the level from which Marxist theory erupts is not the level of intellectual and contemplative "genius"; it is the level of revolutionary practice.

A *philosopher of Marxism*, therefore, should understand how to enact *Marxist philosophy* by not confusing their philosophical commitments with the science that enabled the existence of these commitments. None of this is to say that the Marxist canon should be approached religiously, as a set of sacred texts that only need to be properly interpreted and applied (for this approach, after all, is the result of the mechanical understanding of *Marxist philosophy*), but that any valid re-interrogation of the core concepts is the province of revolutionary science, not philosophy, and that this revolutionary science can only emerge from world historical revolutionary processes—not from philosophical contemplation.[14]

Indeed, the main reason I have cited Althusser is because, as much as I have significant philosophical disagreements with various aspects of his work, he was one of the few philosophers who understood the role of philosophy and its relationship with the object of Marxism. He properly understood the role of philosophy vis-a-vis Marxism, did not confuse philosophy with theory, was precise in his philosophical investigations and interpretations of debates and problematics within the universe he took as his object (Marxism), and established philosophical concepts that were *properly* philosophical concepts— philosophical concepts designed to clarify the boundaries of that which could be called Marxist science. If we must disagree with Althusser we cannot do so because he misunderstood the relationship of philosophy to Marxism but that, to invert one of his aphorisms, he was sometimes giving the wrong answers to the right questions.[15] The point, however, is that he is one of the few philosophers working in the field of Marxism who understood the questions; he correctly described how to begin, a position that is difficult for so many Marxists who are also philosophers to grasp. He understood the interpretative and investigative role of philosophy, the fact that to perform philosophy as a Marxist is not to perform revolutionary science, and that (perhaps most importantly) "only 'the militants of the revolutionary class struggle' to really grasp the thought of the process in relations. Therefore, genuine thought of [Marxist] process is possessed by those engaged in political practice."[16]

In any case, I have chosen to stress the use of *the philosophy of Marxism* over *Marxist philosophy* because I believe that the former statement expresses the proper role of philosophy while the latter might lead to what was warned against by Marx's eleventh thesis. Sometimes we encounter the kind of Marxist philosopher who, rather than accept that they are simply interpreting the world, believes that through their contemplative exercises they are somehow engaged in a world historical process. And as a philosopher who is also a communist I believe that those of us who practise philosophy as Marxists—if we actually want to abide by what the Marxist problematic demands—need to stop confusing revolutionary philosophy with revolutionary science.

Making sense of the world

I have chosen to connect interpretation to investigation because to interpret something requires, one would hope, an investigation into this something's terms of existence. That which is not investigated cannot be properly interpreted: one cannot imagine, after all, someone interpreting a book from one language into another without first investigating the terms of the language they are interpreting. To go further, interpretation/ investigation necessarily means intervention and demarcation. An investigation, if it is successful, will not only intervene on a given problematic but result in an interpretive gesture that, by declaring meaning, necessarily demarcates itself from other interpretations. The process of investigation-interpretation-intervention-demarcation demonstrates that philosophy is that which attempts to make sense of the world; it is concerned with meaning and is thus the practice of denouement.

Although we could argue that every academic discipline is, in some way or another, an attempt to make sense of the world, philosophy is the only discipline that, in itself, is primarily concerned with the question of making sense. The theoretical physicist, after all, does not need to concern themself with whether or not their theorems make sense to the lay person, and especially not the historical procession of meanings behind their discipline. Whenever the second-order question "what does this mean"—or, more specifically, "what does this mean in the world"—is raised, then one has already passed, if only marginally (and usually, when practised by those trained in other modes of thought, the passage is very marginal indeed), into the realm of philosophy which should be the realm of rigorous interpretation, of investigation, of contemplating the terms of meaning.

Indeed, the three "traditional" branches of philosophy— ontology, epistemology, ethics—are primarily concerned with meaning. "What does it mean to exist?" or "what does it mean to be?" are the questions that define ontology/metaphysics. Epistemology generally asks "what does it mean to know?", its inquiry concerned with the meaning of knowledge. And the questions concerning ethics are "what does it mean to be good [or bad]?" and "what is the meaning of goodness [or badness]?" All of these questions are attempts to make sense of the world, to excavate the meaning of the world, but are also moments of interpretation, investigation, and not of change.

The problem noted by Marx in the eleventh thesis, however, is that sometimes attempts to make sense of the world, to interpret meaning through speculative investigation, are often mistaken, even if unconsciously, with engaging in changing the world. In *Theses on Feuerbach* Marx was beginning to separate himself from a confused tradition that treated philosophical questions as questions concerning change rather than interpretation: as a materialist he could no longer approach the world as an object of alienated thought—which was a confusion philosophers such as Feuerbach were making—that could be changed by properly understanding what it meant for the world to be humanized. Although I differ with Althusser on a variety of areas that are outside the gamut of this project, I believe he was quite correct in arguing that philosophical preoccupations with this concept have nothing to do with changing the world. Humanism (not to be confused, in my opinion, with philosophical questions regarding what it means to be human) is a philosophical dead-end for those who take historical and dialectical materialism to be their starting point.

Earlier I claimed that the eleventh thesis on Feuerbach might signify a rupture with the way in which philosophy has been understood as a practice and thus *opens a critique of the way philosophy has historically understood itself while simultaneously suggesting that philosophy has always been, and can only be, something other than its illusions.* By now, based on my philosophical propositions and the ensuing discussion, this claim should be clear: although philosophy has always been only that which can interpret the world—an investigation of a specific object in order to ask questions connected to meaning—the history of philosophy indicates that philosophers have tended to imagine, and still imagine, that they are involved in something larger than the simple act of investigating circumstances.

The emergence of historical materialism resulted in a demystification of philosophy: if social practice, rather than ideas produced by social practice, was understood as the primary motor of historical change, then philosophy—which was always about ideas and contemplation—also needed to be understood as something other than it had imagined itself to be. The assumption on the part of philosophers that everything was the object of philosophy, that contemplating the world according to abstract categories of thought unified the world through the "queen of the disciplines", was challenged: grand philosophical systems are produced by social practice and, in the last instance, have really been nothing more than interpretative gestures that are often unaware of themselves as such. The world is not unified through contemplation.

Here again, Althusser is salient:

In order to make all social practices and ideas enter its

domain, and in order to impose itself upon these social practices and ideas with the aim of speaking their truth for them, philosophy plays tricks. That is, when philosophy absorbs and re-elaborates them in accordance with its own philosophical form, it scarcely does it with scrupulous respect for the reality (the particular nature) of such social practices and ideas.[17]

Althusser goes on to claim that philosophy as it has been traditionally understood has refused to understand that it possesses an "exterior space" and, by assuming that it is "queen of the sciences", has failed to recognize that it is simply interpreting the world. In this way philosophy also attempts to comprehend historical change, misunderstands philosophical investigation as synonymous with change, and thus fails to miss the point of changing the world. Marx's demystification of thought, however, "introduce[s] the scandalous fracture of practice into the very heart of philosophy".[18]

And yet even those of us who understand the need to break from the grand philosophical projects of the past are, in some ways, still unable to grasp Marx's demystification of thought: academic Marxists in general, and philosophers specifically, are often guilty of imagining that their academic work is synonymous with changing the world—that to interpret the world, to write a book on this-or-that theoretical problem, is revolutionary praxis. Such work, however, is not by itself political; if it was, based on the amount of books and papers published, capitalism would have already collapsed under the weight of academic rigour. Philosophy, because of its long history of being treated as the basis for both theory and existence, is the worst offender: every time it is displaced it finds ways to reassert itself as a new ontological condition.

In *Conditions* Badiou proclaims:

After submitting the history of philosophy to philosophical examination, almost all our contemporaries agree to say that this history has entered the—perhaps interminable—era of its closure. Philosophy is thus affected by malaise and what I shall term a delocalization: it no longer knows if it has a proper place. As a result, it either strives to graft itself onto established activities—art, poetry, science, political action, psychoanalysis and so on—or *merely* passes over into its own history, becoming a museum of itself.[19]

But rather than recognize that his above assessment might indicate the closure of the understanding of philosophy that pre-existed the Marxist rupture, and that this is cause for celebration, Badiou worries about "[t]he prevailing idea that metaphysics is historically depleted",[20] which is why he will embark on a project to re-establish philosophy as an ontological system. The final statement of the *Tractatus* thus can only be understood as "sophistry"[21] (which, to be fair, is an honest way to read it solely in light of Wittgenstein's project), and thus can "never be an interpretation of experience. It involves the act of Truth with regard to truths."[22] Philosophy's primary authority is thus reestablished as an "act of Truth". What is odd, however, is that just before he reinstates the idealist conception of philosophy that does not understand that the philosophical practice can only be about interpreting the world—dismissing the practice of interpretation despite sublimating it within lofty metaphysical language—Badiou makes an assertion that signals the practice of philosophy in the shadow of the eleventh thesis: "[p]hilosophy is prescribed by conditions that constitute types of truth- or generic-procedure".[23] These conditions are science, art (specifically poetry), politics, and love. While we can dispense with the limited conditional names he provides,[24] we should recognize that he briefly indicates a reversal where the practice of philosophy is prescribed by pre-existing truth procedures.

Badiou should have stuck with this statement and traced out its meaning rather than reestablishing philosophy qua-philosophy.

Indeed, what Badiou indicated about philosophy, before embracing an idealist recapture of its meaning, was that it was not synonymous with particular conditions, or zones of theory. The latter generate truth procedures. The former is prescribed by these theoretical conditions. Philosophy is not synonymous with theory. In some ways it possesses less importance than the work of the political economist or social theorist. In order to put philosophy properly in its place, and thus avoid the confusion that results from a common conflation of philosophy with theory, it will be necessary to examine its relationship with theory.

Notes

1. Meaning a process wherein insights/discoveries lead to other insights/discoveries in a complex dialectic over long historical periods.

2. Meillassoux, echoing Bertrand Russell, has also indicated that Kant's so-called "Copernican Revolution" might have in fact been a "Ptolemaic Counter-Revolution" in that it recentred the human world after this world was judged to *not* be the centre of the universe by the new sciences.

3. Lazarus, 80. We should note, however, that Lazarus, finding himself in the shadow of this "break" and understanding its historical importance, is also devoted to arguing for a successive break from the kind of "classist" [meaning classificatory, not the pejorative term of upper class chauvinism towards workers] scientism of which Marxism is a part. Although a direct and thorough critique of Lazarus' project is beyond the scope of my book, the arguments I will present regarding the "political decision" will provide their own immanent critique.

4. Marx and Engels, *The German Ideology*, 42.

5. Marx and Engels, *The German Ideology*, 571.

6. Morera, *Gramsci, Materialism, and Philosophy*, 13.
7. Although, as discussed earlier, I have borrowed the term "philosophical decision" from François Laruelle, I am not in agreement with his project. I will discuss this in a later section of the book.
8. Shaw, 25.
9. As will become clear in a later chapter, I understand *class* in an intersectional rather than essentialist sense. That is, class struggle necessarily implies multiple sites of oppression such as race, gender, ability, etc.
10. Badiou, *Metapolitics*, 16.
11. Badiou, *Polemics*, 4.
12. Althusser, *For Marx*, 33.
13. Ibid., 33-34.
14. In *Continuity and Rupture* I attempted to demarcate the logic of such an emergence.
15. Althusser famously claimed that the students of May 1968 in Paris were "giving the right answers to the wrong questions".
16. Badiou, *Metapolitics*, 60. The importance of Althusser in regards to this project will be discussed in a later chapter.
17. Althusser, *Philosophy and the Spontaneous Philosophy of the Scientists*, 250.
18. Ibid., 251.
19. Badiou, *Conditions*, 3.
20. Ibid.
21. Ibid., 6.
22. Ibid., 24.
23. Ibid., 23.
24. For example, why is *poetry* accorded such importance in the realm of the arts in a context where poetry is generally outmoded, and the arts as a whole comprise cinema, modern installations, contemporary music, and a whole host of other forms that generate more meaning than poetry? There is a

holdover, here, from the ancients that has found its way into French philosophy. On the one hand, contemporary French philosophers tend to place too much importance on poets such as Mallarmé at the expense of the cultural sphere as a whole. On the other hand, the philosophy of antiquity was obsessed with poetry because it was the primary expression of literature. Badiou's obsession with Plato unifies these two valorizations of poetry. We do not have enough time to explore the exceptional status given to poetry—an exceptional status that is generated by a Eurocentric obsession with an Athenian origin of philosophy—just as we do not have time to explore the odd reasons that "love" is given pride of place.

Chapter Two

philosophy and the theoretical terrain

Philosophy is the invention of strange forms of argumentation, necessarily bordering on sophistry, which remains its dark structural double. To philosophize is always to develop an idea whose elaboration and defence require a novel kind of argumentation, the model for which lies neither in positive science – not even in logic – nor in some supposedly innate faculty for proper reasoning. Thus it is essential that a philosophy produce internal mechanisms for regulating its own inferences – signposts and criticisms through which the newly constituted domain is equipped with a set of constraints that provide internal criteria for distinguishing between licit and illicit claims.
Quentin Meillassoux, After Finitude

In order to make sense of philosophy's relationship with theory and the difference between these terms (as claimed by the third proposition of the preceding chapter) I will employ the metaphor of a *terrain* wherein the practice of philosophy is an intervention upon the presented geography of theory. The employment of this metaphor/analogy will be useful for the remainder of this book's intervention, a way in which to conceptualize the problematic of philosophical practice. Since no analogies are perfect, and extended metaphors will always reach their limits, this comparison is simply intended to distinguish philosophy from theory while noting their connection. Although it is correct to assert that philosophy is not the same as theory, it is also important to note that the former would not be possible without the latter and, conversely, the latter often requires the former in order to provide clarity.

Since the cartographer is someone who interprets the world

according to the model of the map, the metaphor of *terrain* is useful for explaining how philosophy interacts with a world of theory: the world is already presented to the cartographer; the map is an intervention, a drawing of routes and boundaries. Similarly, theory is already presented to the philosopher; philosophy is also an intervention, a charting of lines of clarity and demarcation, that, like the map, is a denouement machine that forces meaning.

What is a theoretical terrain?

A theoretical terrain is the result of an historical process. Presented to us by history, emerging from history's motion, a theoretical terrain is determined by class struggle. Therefore, a given body of theory does not come into existence without struggle. Those responsible for expressing the terrain and its boundaries, after all, are embedded in concrete social and historical circumstances: they are not pure Hegelian souls; their ideas, when organized, form the topography of a given theoretical terrain and are bound to their lived, social/historical activity.

A theoretical terrain is an organized body of conceptual thought that attempts to make sense of reality. A theoretical terrain may also contain sub-terrains, or provinces, that possess their own boundaries. Provinces can be apprehended as their own theoretical terrains, when necessary and for the sake of coherence, which is why it is possible to speak of the theoretical terrain of "religion" and the theoretical terrain of "Christianity" although it is also true that the latter is a province of the former. What matters is the coherence of the boundaries: a theoretical terrain is that which is understood, and has been historically presented to us, as a body of theory with a comprehensible identity.

Being an organized body of theory that attempts to make sense of reality, a theoretical terrain could be religious or scientific, idealist or materialist, irrational or rational, and anything that passes for a coherent body of theory. Theoretical terrains that are scientific (and thus materialist) are the most important because they make sense of reality in a manner that other theoretical terrains, regardless of their aspirations, are incapable of providing. And yet scientific terrains are the most difficult to grasp because the nature of scientific truth is *procedural*—it is always open to the future, mediated by historical production— and so the boundaries of such terrains, while possessing general characteristics that appear the same, are always in flux. To be fair, the exteriority of most theoretical terrains, scientific or not, are in flux because they are historical constructs and history is change. Scientific terrains, however, openly recognize that change is immanent.

Most importantly, a theoretical terrain that is demonstrably scientific concerns the process of truth and proves this concern through its historical effects. No other type of theoretical terrain possesses the same claim to truth; those terrains that set themselves up in opposition to science are either idealist or a terrain consisting of *theory-for-the-sake-of-theory* that, by itself, lacks truth value (and is sometimes proud of this lack).

None of this is to say that terrains lacking the same truth claim as those terrains that are "scientific" are without worth. There are, for example, aesthetic terrains that may possess their own interior truth procedures, accruing over various historical periods, that require intervention: the historical working out of art, film, and literature, while not evincing scientific truth claims, may be no less important. The theoretical inscriptions of these concerns are terrains that also demand engagement because, as with science, they emerge from social practice.

Above all, a theoretical terrain is a metaphor imagined for the sake of philosophical clarity.

The condition of the terrain

To practise philosophy is to engage in cartography—to explore and map the geography of a given terrain. This practice always involves fidelity, conscious or unconscious, to one or more theoretical terrain that might not be the terrain under investigation. Take, for example, philosophical interventions on the terrain of medical science that are driven by a post-modern suspicion of science in general: such a mapping will transpose the geography of another terrain upon the one that is being explored in order to make sense of the latter.

Hence, the practice of philosophy results in the drawing and redrawing of multiple routes within a given terrain. Moreover, philosophy is that which attempts to demarcate a terrain's boundaries as well as the boundaries of its sub-terrains, or what even counts as a province in the first place. All philosophical demarcations and routes lack neutrality; like the theoretical terrains themselves, these interventions are conditioned by the motion of history—class struggle—and this declaration, it needs to be admitted, is a declaration that *also* lacks neutrality. But presupposing a truth, even if it is the pithy claim that "there is no truth", is not a neutral activity; the category of truth, by definition, cannot be neutral. Truth is that which excludes.

The only condition for philosophy, as with a theoretical terrain, is the motion of history. Here we definitely part with Badiou who, rejecting "historicism", has argued that philosophy's conditions are science, art, politics, and love. But these conditions are the composition of various theoretical terrains, and every theoretical terrain is the product of history's motion. A theoretical terrain is presented to us but this presentation is not eternal: it is the product of real people producing in concrete historical circumstances.

Mapping a theoretical terrain involves declaring what does or does not belong to its landscape according to the logic of its boundaries. What provinces and topographical elements are an organic part of the terrain; what provinces are occupying colonies, invasions that need to be defeated; what elements produce famines of thought and conceptual contagions. Some terrains need to be metaphorically decolonized, or at least properly re-articulated.

Philosophical line struggle is thus the drawing of lines within a given terrain so as to respond to enemy lines of demarcation. Lines are first drawn through the terrain's exterior boundaries, so as to apprehend the general meaning, and then drawn as routes and interior boundaries: the topography and geography is reconceptualized. If the terrain is scientific then this philosophical line struggle must wage war on all attempts to distort the exterior boundaries and, in this distortion, the mapping of terrible routes and provinces that deform the geography as a whole.

We know of the distortions that were thankfully defeated in other scientific terrains by those who were able to correctly apprehend the boundaries and, following this apprehension, mark the appropriate routes of truth's procession. In the terrain of physics we were once faced with the divergent mappings of the Newtonian or Leibnizian paradigm; the militant struggle in this terrain of science, however, transformed the former paradigm into a province at the expense of the latter. Correctly apprehending a terrain's boundaries, as they have been presented by history, is necessary: theorists developing these terrains do so on a regular basis; philosophers, who are often lagging behind, tend to declare their allegiance to a particular theorist or theoretical province and, in this declaration, clarify a given terrain according to this allegiance so as to end up on the right or wrong side of history.

Thus a theoretical terrain develops with or without the intervention of philosophy. In the drawing of routes and boundaries philosophy attempts to provide clarity, but it might provide clarity for an archaic topography, a geographic structure relegated to the past by the logic of the terrain's boundaries. And yet philosophy can play an important role in providing this clarity: the drawing of routes, of demarcating lines, forces meaning.

Indeed, this exercise in constructing an extended metaphor of a *terrain* is itself an example of the practice of philosophy. Imagining a *theoretical terrain* is nothing more than a useful model of reality designed to make sense of (to clarify, to force meaning) theory and philosophy's relationship to theory. Hence, this is not a theory about theory—after all, theory does not exist as a concrete assemblage of geography in the real world—but an exercise that is meant to demonstrate the practical function of philosophy. Since it is a model intended to demonstrate philosophy's function, it should not be treated as a meta-theoretical truth; like most analogies, its use is in its ability to force meaning but it is not meaning in and of itself.

Fidelity and the terrain

Obviously this model of the *theoretical terrain* is conditioned by my own fidelity to Marxism. But I have already admitted to this conditioning and, most importantly, I have argued that all philosophical interventions within a given terrain can never be neutral. We can imagine another narration of this model in which the narrator is not a Marxist, and thus does not develop the argument in order to address the problematic of the Marxist terrain; but within this imaginary, subtracting the points conditioned by historical materialism, the metaphor would still hold. That is, this is a model that describes the practice of philosophy and the only reason I have described this practice according to historical materialist categories—even beginning by arguing that theoretical terrains are the reflection of class struggle—is because neutrality is impossible. Theoretical fidelity is already proscribed in the description of philosophical practice.

To be conditioned by one's political fidelity, however, is to also be conditioned by history since our ideology is the effect of the social and historical position(s) we occupy. Our relationship to a theoretical terrain is derived from our position in class struggle and how we interpret the meaning of this positionality: what classes and relations of force we align ourselves with, what ideology determines our consciousness. As I noted in the previous chapter, specifically in my fourth proposition regarding Marx's eleventh thesis, philosophy cannot escape class commitments.

The practice of philosophy, the intervention on a given theoretical terrain, is not found in an ahistorical box containing unconditioned tools that, once applied to the terrain in question, will produce the same answers if utilized correctly. Even the instruments of formal logic, that some positivists once imagined to be purely unconditioned, cannot achieve perfect consensus when applied to the same theoretical terrain—which is why analytic philosophers have been arguing over the smallest regions in theoretical terrains for decades without reaching the kind of agreement that a set of Platonic instruments should produce. Hence the infinite debates over normative ethics where each philosopher utilizes precisely the same tools and accuses the others of faulty reasoning to the point that all or none are guilty of using their tools poorly.

None of this is to make the dubious claim that there is no such thing as the truth but only that all attempts to apprehend the process of truth in a specific terrain are conditioned by the motion of history which is itself an unavoidable truth. The philosopher, however, cannot assume that they can transcend their historical circumstances simply because of their disciplinary training. Rather, philosophers are simply engaged in drawing routes with recourse to the tool box that they have inherited which may in fact be a terrain in and of itself.

Therefore, since philosophy is the only discipline capable of taking itself as an object (for if any other terrain took itself as its own object it would immediately be performing, by the very definition of this act, philosophy), we can also speak of a moment where philosophy itself becomes a theoretical terrain. In becoming a theoretical terrain in its own right, however, philosophy is no longer philosophy-qua-philosophy but simply a reflection of philosophical practice that has ossified into a potential theory so as to allow for further philosophical practice. Take, for example, formal logic which is meant to be a methodology of political practice, used to draw routes in a given terrain; once it is treated as a terrain in itself it becomes something that is presented by the motion of history, a complex geography that *is*, and the same methodology that is used to trace second-order routes across this terrain, which might at first seem recursive, is the act of philosophy.

Perhaps a creative way of interpreting Wittgenstein's conclusion in the *Tractatus*— "[w]hat we cannot speak about we must pass over in silence"[1]—is as an illustration of theoretical terrains and the lines of demarcation marked by philosophy. For if philosophy is nothing more than the tracing of routes through a given theoretical terrain, its authority to speak is limited: the tracing is often a silent *passing over* that leaves lines of demarcation; when we must speak it is only in fidelity to what has already been presented but what we have come to recognize as integral to the terrain we are exploring. And, in any case, only the theoretical terrain "speaks" in presenting us with a body of knowledge that we are led to investigate and, in investigating, force further moments of "speaking".

The Marxist terrain

When it comes to the terrain of Marxism, as with every theoretical terrain, we find a complex palimpsest of routes, provinces and landscapes which are all defended according to the purported logic of this terrain's boundaries. The role of the philosopher of Marxism (as with the philosopher of physics) is to chart a coherent route through this treacherous terrain. Better yet, to use this route and this mapping as the basis for a theoretical people's war upon those elements that might be grasped as sites of occupation.

In the history of real-world cartography just as there were those who developed this skill in order to make sense of the geographies in which they lived or to which they possessed fidelity, there were also those whose drawing of boundaries and routes was in the service of conquest, imperialism, and the division of peoples. The former group intended their mapping to produce clarification for both themselves and others who shared or enjoyed the geography they were attempting to illuminate. The latter group, prominent in the period of modern colonialism, was interested in only illuminating routes of conquest so as to ultimately disarticulate the terrain they were mapping.

Thus there are philosophers who have mapped the Marxist terrain who, lacking fidelity to this terrain's boundaries, are similar to the colonial cartographer. The routes they have left demonstrate loyalty to hostile, or at the very least suspicious, theoretical terrains. Hence, as with the religious mystic's attempt to chart the terrains of "natural" science, these philosophical interventions produce confusion; their effects need to be apprehended, combatted, or erased.

At the same time, however, belonging to the school of cartography that possesses fidelity to the terrain under investigation does not guarantee precision: one can be a terrible cartographer who, despite one's intentions, provides confusing and misleading maps. So there are also Marxist philosophers who map this terrain in a divergent manner: competing provinces are declared, various routes are emphasized at the expense of others, the characteristics of the terrain's landscape are debated. Sometimes, even these routes that are mapped in fidelity to the terrain's boundaries echo hostile cartographies— hence those Marxist delineations of the provincial geography of "Stalinism" that is amplified only to be effaced, but according to a delineation previously performed by imperial cartographers.

Those of us who believe, against current academic fashion, that the terrain of Marxism is a *scientific* terrain are further forced to militantly defend these boundaries according to the concept of scientific truth. Like the militants of other scientific terrains and provinces that have fought to prove their historical veracity, philosophical intervention on the terrain of Marxism necessarily struggles against dogmatism and revisionism. For every scientific terrain produces its own variants and combinations of dogmatism and revisionism: there will be those who refuse to recognize developing provinces, new sub-terrains, within their field because it calls all of their assumptions into question; there will be those who want to invent new provinces that contradict the overall terrain's boundaries; there will be those who desire to reprogram the entire terrain based on a mythical purity of its logic and, in so doing, refuse to recognize that a scientific terrain, by virtue of being scientific, is open to the future—a dogmatism that is also a revisionism because it rejects the logic of the terrain's exterior boundaries.

Conceptualizing Marxism as a theoretical terrain that is also scientific, however, produces a level of coherence that is missing from all other conceptualizations of Marxism. For to act under the assumption that Marxism is not scientific is to concede that every province and route is correct as long as it maintains the most banal fidelity to the exterior boundaries: along with the likes of Paul Hirst and Barry Hindess we could say that the theoretical terrain of Marxism lacks definitive boundaries altogether and is thus open to every revisionist mapping that names itself *Marxist*. Since the philosopher of a scientific terrain that takes science seriously would never make such a claim about physics, biology, chemistry, etc.—and thus begins their intervention from the position that there is something that makes these terrains distinct and that this something determines the terrain's evolution—to assert that Marxism is also a scientific terrain is to subtract the attempted interventions of those who would render it incoherent.

Moreover, apprehending Marxism as a scientific terrain

allows for a level of clarity that would otherwise be non-existent. If we argue that the exterior boundaries of the Marxist terrain are scientific boundaries then we are immediately concerned with the procedure of truth that will affect all of our interior demarcations. As with any science, we are forced to establish the truth process that is particular to this terrain and such an establishment provides further clarity: Marxism, or *historical materialism*, is the science of history/society which asserts that class revolution is the motive force of history/society. If we are to map interior routes and boundaries according to this exterior demarcation, then we will be forced to concede that class revolution is the foundational logic of our cartography. All routes and provinces should only be drawn according to the logic of this science; everything that is not a result of world historical revolutions and the revolutionary movements produced by these singular moments should be deleted from our mapping.

Hence the singularity of Marxism-Leninism-Maoism: three provinces, terrains in and of themselves, that exist according to the scientific logic of the general terrain's boundaries. If the boundaries of the Marxist theoretical terrain are understood as scientific, and this science of history is taken seriously, this can be the only result of a philosophical intervention that proceeds from such premises. The truth procedure of the terrain has produced these sub-terrains according to its exterior logic; only if we reject this terrain's scientific status can we argue otherwise.[7]

Such a mapping provides a coherence, according to the boundaries, that is otherwise lost in the innumerable and often myopic attempts to explore this terrain. Fidelity to this coherence necessitates a metaphorical people's war within the terrain, a philosophical militancy that is aimed at erasing and effacing those routes and boundaries that are alien to the overall logic. Inversely, fidelity to an incoherent interpretation of the terrain's boundaries places the philosophy of Marxism in a position of dogmatism, revisionism, or a combination of these two categories: routes and boundaries that defy the scientific logic of the terrain's exteriority will be drawn in a defiant act of colonial cartography.

And yet even with this general rearticulation of the terrain's geography there is still much that needs to be investigated: the distinction between these three general provinces, the meaning of the most recent province, the relation between the three that is both continuous and discontinuous, and the possibility of further provincial emergences. If anything, the model of the *terrain* should help us understand how these provincial moments in the overall theoretical terrain can and should be investigated as (sub)terrains in and of themselves.

Philosophy and the terrain

As with any terrain, there will be mappings of Marxism that forget they are only mappings, and thus pretend they are producing the terrain itself. Philosophical intervention does not produce theory; the terrain's development is not the result of those interventions that act as if they are presenting the landscape's truth procedure simply by proclaiming that an overwriting of the terrain is correct simply by the act of marking routes. In the history of literal map-making, after all, there are innumerable examples of false cartographies that have attempted to proclaim a terrain's existence by recourse to an imaginary model: maps to El Dorado, of the kingdom of Prester John, and other fevered colonial fantasies that simulated real terrains.

A terrain emerges and develops through an historical process that philosophy must apprehend; the terrain of Marxism is presented to us, ready to map, by a succession of revolutions, specifically world historical revolutions, in which a geography is concretized. It is the business of philosophy to make sense of this emergence and development, to work with what is already presented, rather than pretend it is engaged in forcing this emergence and development. The primary thing that is forced through the drawing of routes and boundaries is clarity and a choice of meaning, not the theoretical terrain itself. The question philosophers of Marxism should be trying to answer is: *what is the interior meaning of this terrain, at this historical juncture, and what choices does it present us with?* Not: *what is the geography that we can create within a set of boundaries that we can also imagine?* Whereas the former question allows for honest philosophical investigation and intervention, the latter question results in academic eclecticism and the simulation of Marxism's truth process.

More than simply being a misleading act of cartography, this simulating type of intervention tends to resemble the hostile route drawing of the colonial cartographer in that it tends to deform the geography and neutralize its truth procedure. Imagine, here, the well-intentioned philosopher of mathematics who, despite not being a mathematician, attempts to tell mathematicians the meaning of their terrain and, confusing philosophical investigation with science itself, acting as if they can determine the foundational meaning of the terrain, the basis of mathematics itself...If any mathematician took such a philosopher seriously then the science itself would be hampered and confined by the intervention.

Unfortunately, many Marxist militants are often distracted by the musings of Marxist philosophers who pretend, though separated from what produces their theoretical terrain, that they can provide this terrain with its foundations. Just as mathematics is better off without the direction of philosophers of maths, Marxism is better off without the direction of philosophers of Marxism. Both can be *served*, however, by these same philosophers as long as they understand that their proper role is to draw routes and boundaries through what is already presented.

In the end, the practice of philosophy should be properly understood as an act of service to the theoretical terrain in which philosophy is being enacted. The faithful cartographer has always placed themself in service to the geography they are attempting to illuminate. Being faithful to this geography should mean the rejection of any fidelity to a project that intends to deform a theoretical terrain: we must remember that colonial cartographers were faithful first and foremost to colonialism above the project of cartography—this historical fact should guide our understanding of the metaphor of the theoretical terrain.

Therefore, to ask the question *what is a theoretical terrain?* is to also ask the question *what is philosophy?* and, in this asking, to force a connection between these two moments of inquiry. A theoretical terrain is presented to us through the momentum of history; philosophy investigates this terrain as an act of service. There should be no aggrandization of the latter at the expense of the former.

The terrain as metaphor

I want to emphasize again that the theoretical terrain is a metaphor: it is not ontological in the grand sense, either as a transcendent concept that exists somewhere, outside of space in time, as a supervening principle, nor is it an immanent law of nature. Rather, the terrain is simply a model of thought designed to explain philosophical intervention. As a philosophical model, it is an interpretive gesture in and of itself. There are no literal theoretical terrains that we can discover, the boundaries of which can ever be perfectly described.

Hence, the terrain is useful insofar as it can help us understand the relationship between philosophy and theory—that is, to help us *think philosophy* or, more accurately, understand the philosophy of philosophy. Beyond the general description of this model we should not waste time providing formulae that can help us mathematically or logically describe particular terrains and thus produce a precise geography with clear borders that always demarcate one known terrain from another. Instead, we should use the concept of the terrain as a rough guide to thought.

There may be times when, using this model, it makes sense to treat several related theories as regions within a larger terrain; there may be other times where it makes sense to treat these theoretical trajectories as terrains unto themselves. The decision of how to apprehend a terrain is a philosophical decision, the result of which might provide us with different problematics. Indeed, one philosophical decision might lead us to divide theory into the extremely general terrains of *religion*, *art*, and *science*—these are, after all, traditional ways in which philosophy has conceptualized thought and, due to this conceptualization, has succeeded in making some successful and historical interventions. At the same time, however, it may make sense to treat these three terrains as general continents wherein which other terrains reside with distinct boundaries and separate truth procedures: multiple scientific terrains, multiple artistic terrains, multiple religious terrains. Physics is not necessarily the same terrain as biology, though we can in some sense imagine that this is the case, nor is surrealism the same as symbolism.

Treating a terrain as a sub-terrain, or vice versa, is simply a decision that allows us, through the model as a whole, to demarcate a particular theoretical logic and, in this demarcation, attempt to isolate its internal procedures. Sometimes an overlap is useful; other times demarcation is necessary. When should we treat physics and biology as the same terrain? When we are speaking of the logic of science, as opposed to mysticism, in general. When should we treat these same sciences as two separate terrains? When we are looking at the particular and different truth procedures that necessarily mean different frameworks for making sense of existence. Even understanding when, how, and why to (re)conceptualize multiple terrains is a philosophical decision.

The practice of cartography is an apt metaphor because it

performs the same function upon concrete geographies. Where does one terrain begin and another end in the reality modelled by a map? Between nations, continents, provinces, cities, districts, blocks? They are all a single terrain; they are simultaneously multiple terrains. The lines are in one sense imaginary, in another sense very real: we do not see the 49th parallel drawn across the North American continent as a literal line; we know it is real in the sense that it is maintained by two nation-states who have decided, based on different national logics, the colonial division of one larger terrain into two separate and supposedly distinct terrains.

More importantly, though, is the fact that a map is never identical to the terrain it attempts to represent. Referring to a story by Borges, Jean Baudrillard tried to problematize the idea of the map, of the model, by arguing that no model could properly account for reality without becoming reality itself.[3] In some ways, this was a tactic designed to attack scientific logic, specifically historical materialism, that reduced reality to a model so as to discover, at an abstract level, particular truths. By assuming that this could never be done—reality cannot be reduced to a model without the model becoming reality itself (the map is the terrain, simply super-imposed), and thus functionally useless, Baudrillard would flee into the cold embrace of nihilism.

And yet the map does not pretend to be reality itself, and to dismiss scientific abstraction because it does not accord to the crudest and most apparent empiricism, represents a typical confusion of a *model* with an *ontological system*. Although I plan to discuss this confusion in more detail at a later point, let me provide a few brief remarks that will serve to conclude this chapter.

While it is correct to recognize that some models are confused with ontological systems, and that this has hampered thought for centuries, to dispense with models simply because they are models (or *simulacra*) is to become the enemy of thought itself.

A map works because, if it is followed and we understand its instructions, we can chart our course in a terrain with which we might lack familiarity. A map fails when it cannot interpret the terrain in which we are operating. This is the only meaning that matters, and this is why the notion of the terrain is a useful metaphor: demarcating lines, boundaries of thought, direction of meaning. Thus, the terrain is nothing more than a philosophical metaphor while, at the same time, philosophy would not exist without that which it can imagine and model as a terrain.

This imagining and modelling of the terrain, however, is a contentious practice. To demarcate the terrain according to a particular logic is to simultaneously demarcate oneself from other cartographies. Intervention upon the terrain occludes other types of interventions; to draw a particular line, to make a specific interpretative gesture, is always determined by fidelity to the political decision, even if it is unconscious. That is, the practice of philosophy is always a struggle.

Notes

1. Wittgenstein, §7
2. Indeed, the main reason I was drawn to Maoism was because of a philosophical investigation of the terrain of Marxism that took its core conception of "science" seriously. My reason for conceptualizing theory in terms of the metaphor of *terrain* is, admittedly, also an attempt to reconstruct how I ended up recognizing that Marxism-Leninism-Maoism was unavoidable and logically necessitated by the truth procedure promised by historical materialism. I investigated this in detail in *Continuity and Rupture*.
3. Baudrillard, 1.

Chapter Three

philosophy and struggle

At its best, philosophy liberates. However, because hegemony involves the organization of consensus from the point of view of a dominant social group, and as such is built on the particular interests of a class rather than on universal human interests, philosophy can play a dual role: it can defend particular interests as if they were universal, or it can develop a critique of the false universality of the common sense on which hegemony depends. In short, philosophy may represent the particular interest of a dominant social group or class, or it can represent the interests of those living on the margins of history.
Esteve Morera, Gramsci, Materialism, and Philosophy

Since this book is not simply about the meaning of philosophy but the meaning of the philosophy of Marxism, it is worth investigating how and why I drew a demarcating line that was marked by fidelity to a particular ideology. After all, although Marxism is a terrain that is concerned with social and historical matters, there are clearly other theoretical terrains that compete for ascendancy in the same problematic (liberalism, post-modernism/post-structuralism, etc.), and so to favour Marxism (or, more accurately, *historical materialism*) over one of these competing terrains might seem unjustified.

And yet I would argue that fidelity to other theoretical terrains in the given problematic of *social/historical* is precisely that which lacks justification. For if we are to proceed by favouring, and thus focusing upon, those terrains that are scientific then when it comes to the questions shared by these competing terrains we should gravitate to that terrain that speaks in the language of science, the language of unfolding truths—historical materialism. In the second chapter I alluded to the importance of the Marxist terrain for a philosophy of politics: I indicated that it was scientific and, because it needs to be grasped as scientific, thus resonates with a level of significance lacking in its non-scientific competitors.

Once again we can fall back upon Althusser who, despite his problems, still understood the relationship of philosophy to the emergence of historical materialism:

> Once a genuine knowledge of history had finally been produced, philosophy could no longer ignore, repress or sublimate its relation to history, it had to take account of, and think about, this relation. By means of a theoretical revolution it had to become a new philosophy, capable of thinking—in philosophy itself—its real relation to history, as well as its relation to the truth. The old philosophies of consciousness, of the transcendental subject—just like the dogmatic philosophies of absolute knowledge—were no longer possible philosophically. A new philosophy was necessary, one capable of thinking the *historical insertion* of philosophy in history, its real relation to scientific and social practices.[1]

Historical materialism was thus that scientific terrain that necessitated a transformation in philosophy. I am not only concerned with this necessitation; I am militantly invested in promoting it over other competing philosophical tendencies that, marked by a rejection of the scientific terrain of historical materialism, can provide no significant explanatory depth, consistency, or clarity to the social and historical problematic. Without recourse to that scientific terrain that concerns the object of their critique, these other competing philosophical tendencies are limited to theoretical and practical speculation.

A philosophy that consciously declares fidelity to a scientific terrain produces a practice that, because of its scientific grounding, is concerned with the concrete rather than the speculative. That is, rather than groundlessly ruminating upon life, the universe, and everything without any direction or basis in the real, such a philosophy is primarily concerned with making sense of phenomena according to foundations that are antagonistic to any form of mystification. That which makes the world more confusing, that is not grounded in the processes and structures of actual society, history, and material reality, should be treated as suspect or, at the very least, reinterpreted so as to be placed in relation with the concrete.

(What does a given work of art *mean*, for example, if it is not considered according to how and why this art was produced in a class society, who produced it and who it was produced for, the context of accessibility and gallery structures, and the artist's class position and understanding of class struggle? Even art that imagines itself to be "apolitical" possesses a political function, as the well-known CIA funding of Abstract Expressionism aptly demonstrates. Any philosophical apprehension of a work of art that does not ask these questions is largely speculative, alienated from those concrete practices that permit the production of art in the first place. After all, there is no art or literature that is produced outside of society, by Hegelian pure souls that are free from social-historical *being*, and that can actually be art-for-art's-sake. The best artists understand this fact, especially when they confront art institutions that pretend to be apolitical.[2])

A science is that which explains phenomena according to natural rather than supernatural causes and, in doing so, provides an explanatory depth that is lacking in pseudo-scientific or anti-scientific accounts. Historical materialism satisfies these qualifications when it comes to the phenomena of history and society; the philosophical practice it produces internalizes these concerns and, guided by this logic, is able to draw clear lines of demarcation in every question or problematic in which it is involved. In order to achieve anything that is capable of clarifying thought we need to focus on concrete processes that can be found in the real world. And the concrete processes excavated by historical materialism—the *motion of history*—are processes of class struggle.

Nothing outside of class struggle

No theory or philosophical intervention exists abstractly outside of class struggle, and "in a class society the philosophy so far has been the philosophy of the ruling propertied and exploited class".[3] So when we engage with a given theoretical terrain we encounter two problems: i) the terrain itself, emerging from and developing through an historical process, is affected by the fundamental logic of historical motion, i.e. class struggle; ii) any intervention upon this terrain, any attempt to map and force its meaning, is performed from a position that is embedded within social classes. At first glance this problem, expressed in the fourth proposition of the first chapter, appears insurmountable: after all, if the definition of the terrain's logic as one of "class struggle" is the product of a specific ideology (and if the philosopher intervening upon this terrain does so according to this ideology) then it perhaps makes no sense to speak of objectivity, truth procedures, or anything with universal meaning. That is, if we cannot escape ideology then we should wonder how we can make any judgement or even argue that ideology is inescapable in the first place—an argument that, in itself, represents an ideological position.

Conversely, however, it appears entirely illogical to speak of theories and philosophical judgements that are unconditioned by the real world and thus assume that one can occupy a position of pure objectivity that can only exist outside of space and time. My position, here, is neither new nor entirely controversial; within the critically reflective philosophical tradition, after all, claims of pure objectivity have always been challenged without rejecting the concept of truth claims. Take, for example, Lorraine Code's work in the area of epistemology where assumptions about a purely objective knowledge and a purely objective knower are necessarily called into question. The "presumed political innocence" of such a position, Code argues, "needs to be challenged". And then, paralleling Mao, she states: "[c]ritics must ask who this epistemology is for, whose interests it serves, and whose it neglects or suppresses in the process".[4]

Moreover, those who would have us believe that there is such a thing as an unconditioned objectivity must find themselves trapped in another problem: they themselves are conditioned by their history and yet assume, based only on their say-so, that there is a logic and theory free from the messiness of human interaction. According to this view of reality, a given science's truth value was discovered, as if it was hiding somewhere in the natural world, and the development of this science becomes a reified process free from social relations: it does not need the human theorists, themselves limited by their finite lives and social conditions, but is simply an objective and inhuman process that is working itself out, human theorists be damned.

Thus, if we accept that the developing terrain of any given theory is the result of humans interacting with each other and their existence, and that philosophical intervention is performed by such humans, then we should be forced to also accept the fact that we cannot escape ourselves. Our societies, our histories, and the positions we occupy within a social-historical process matter. Even scientific theory admits that this is the case: we would not be able to explain the paradigm shift from Newton to Einstein if we did not accept that historical context produces moments of rupture; we would not be able to explain all of the ideological dead-ends that science encountered if we could not speak of the ideological moment that conditions every theorist. The phrenologist who once claimed scientific objectivity, for example, can only be explained by identifying the social fact of racism that pre-conditioned scientific investigation.

Furthermore, if we gave up the claim that theory and philosophical intervention are conditioned by history then we would also not be able to make sense of those terrains that are non-scientific. To speak of some unconditioned objectivity in regards to art and literature, for example, leads to a kind of aesthetic philosophy that hasn't changed since the days of Plato and Aristotle where it was assumed that there were perfectly objective concepts of beauty and poetics. This kind of philosophizing about art can tell us nothing about the historical development of art and artistic practice that has developed since the days of the Homeric poems and the dramas of Sophocles. Once we assume that the terrain of art is conditioned by history, however, we can ask whether "Achilles [is] possible with powder and lead? Or the Iliad with the printing press, not to mention the printing machine? Do not the song and the saga and the muse necessarily come to an end with the printer's bar...?"[5] Joseph Conrad's *Heart of Darkness* cannot be rewritten as the same work outside of the context of waning British Empire, its author a subject caught within the crumbling confines of the old imperial order; its possibility has lapsed, regardless of Francis Ford Coppola's attempt to transpose it to the Vietnam War. Similarly, even the faithful replication of the styles of Renaissance visual art today will mean something different, placed within the context of the modern gallery, than they did in the time of the old masters: even if the artist was possessed by a reactionary impulse to embrace old forms and ignore everything that has happened in the art world for the past several centuries, the institution of criticism, art history, and the practice of curation would transform the meaning. What Benjamin called the "aura" of the old works of art,[6] still permitted in museums (institutions dedicated to preserving the old), crumbles in the modern gallery where "mechanical production [has] emancipate[d] the work of art from its parasitical dependence on ritual".[7] Hence,

Gerhard Richter's use of an old style to replicate the Red Army Faction's urban guerrilla activities of *October 1977* (1988) mimic the mechanical reproduction of key photographs, just as his *Two Candles* (1982) intertwines with the reproduction of Sonic Youth's *Daydream Nation* (1988).

In any case, more than simply giving up on this claim about historical conditioning, there is a way out of this supposed contradiction that is not simply a choice between one mistake or its opposite. Although the fact that we are embedded in society and history is inescapable, we do not have to accept that we are overdetermined by social processes—this was the error of Michel Foucault, following Althusser's (historically necessary but ultimately over-stated) rejection of humanism, that led to the self-defeating assumption of a decentered subject.[8] According to this interpretation, we are simply the products of history rather than also being the producers of history and thus cannot locate a position upon which to make judgements: objectivity of any sort is a myth, a self-defeating theory since the very claim about the lack of objectivity is made with objective certainty.

To accept that we cannot escape the fact that we are socially conditioned does not have to mean that our conditioning is total. All it means is that we must be aware of the positions we occupy, conscious of how truth claims are made according to social location, and attempt to transcend these positionalities by interacting with a theoretical terrain with this very understanding in mind.

The history of philosophy-as-such

If philosophy possesses a history, then it is a history of struggle. Even the most anti-Marxist and analytical philosopher should be able to accept that this is the case—after all, what have philosophers been doing except struggling to argue their positions, often by way of *reason*, against those positions they dislike? In every area of philosophy we find articulations of the opposing position so as to establish a counter-position, a desire to found a philosophical ethos, regardless of how rarified, against claims to the contrary. To embark upon the voyage of philosophy is to take a position, to draw demarcating lines around this position, and to dare those who oppose your position to struggle against you.

Hence, in this context, it is worth asking about the origin of such struggle—why are philosophical commitments such that, in order to establish themselves, struggle is required? Why is argument even necessary, why are there opposing views, from what abyss does the fact of such struggle emerge? If the enlightenment philosophers were correct in siding with the natural sciences against a mystified world, then what was the motivation for this siding; conversely, why are philosophers still arguing amongst each other about the positions taken in the so-called enlightenment? These questions indicate a reason and basis for struggle. Without such a reason the internecine struggles of philosophy would be arbitrary, nothing more than a bunch of scholars arguing merely for the reason of argument because they are the type of people "who [go] around with [their] head[s] in the clouds".[9]

The only way to make sense of these struggles, beyond dismissing them as silly arguments of "opinion" between out-of-touch intellectuals, is to locate them in the site of social struggle, i.e. class struggle, that Marx argued was the basis and unavoidable fact of historical development. After all, while it is true that some philosophers are arguing about the same problems that the ancients were arguing about millennia ago (leading to the judgement that philosophy may not possess a history in the same sense that the sciences possess a history), so many philosophical arguments are dependent on facts that could have only been encountered at particular historical moments. One cannot imagine contemporary philosophers of mind discussing problematics raised by the Turing Test—raising questions that could only exist with the conceptualization of the possibility of artificial intelligence—without the historical conditions that would have made the theory of the Turing Test possible in the first place. Parmenides or Descartes, however, would have no reason to examine this problem because they lived in periods where the forces of production were such that these questions about productive relations were inconceivable: no technologies existed so as to challenge our relationship to the problematic of human-made machine consciousness.

The historical fact of class struggle always coincides, to a greater or lesser degree, with philosophy. Such an intersection explains why certain philosophies emerge alongside the ruling ideas of the ruling class, reflecting the "common sense" class hegemony of which Gramsci was concerned. This struggle in the social sphere, which itself drives theoretical transformation, is reflected in the practice of philosophy and may explain why some philosophers found their way into the contemporary canon and others did not.

For example, the historical significance of J.S. Mill for ethical and political philosophy is due, in large part, to the fact that Mill was concretely involved in reforming the bourgeois legal-political order. He is significant insofar as the principle of utility and the principle of liberty are essential to the modern capitalist state. One cannot imagine Mill's arguments on behalf of liberty without the ideology of the free market; without such market reification his so-called "marketplace of ideas" would lack justification. Here we find a philosophical site of struggle bound up in the struggles of the bourgeois order to establish itself.

Indeed, the reduction of normative ethics to a debate between deontology and consequentialism may itself be normative due to the fact that these are simply the only ethical positions permitted by the bourgeois order. On the one hand there is Mill, champion of liberty as utility, but before Mill there was Kant, influenced by the rational order promised by the rise of the bourgeoisie in the French Revolution. An ethical philosophy gleaned from historical materialism merely haunts the borders of this canonical debate, treated as an anachronism because it has only gained recognition due to the level of counter-hegemony it was able to achieve through its long struggles against the established order that produced the ethics of Kant and Mill.

Moreover, the general state of political philosophy is such that the discourse is reduced to a choice between welfare or laissez-faire capitalism: Rawls on one end of the spectrum, Nozick on the other, and a whole host of people in between or trying to replace them. Such a reduction, which intentionally dismisses those who reject this spectrum altogether, results from a social struggle determined by the ideology of those who are interested in preserving the structure of contemporary society. If Marx and those influenced by Marx are to be studied—and they *must* be studied because their impact is undeniable—then they will be marginalized. After all, capitalism conceives of itself as eternal: the economic sphere is taken as a fact of nature; the political sphere, treated as separate from the economic, becomes the concern of social philosophy.

Despite all attempts to inoculate itself from the truth procedure of the Marxist terrain, philosophy has been irrevocably altered by its emergence. Philosophical practice, following this emergence, is revealed precisely for what it has always been: a conflicted history of interpreting the world, and nothing more than innumerable struggles over interpretation and meaning. Marxism puts an end to philosophy-as-such by simultaneously putting it in its proper place: naming it for what it has always been and demanding that all further philosophical interventions be aware of themselves as interventions determined by the logic of class struggle, history and society's momentum.

Philosophers can, of course, deny this insight—and they have. They will continuously labour under the assumption that they are outside of the rupture in thought produced by the Marxist event, embarking on grand projects or limiting themselves to rarified debates. One might as well deny the elementary logic of evolution and particle physics and continue labouring according to this denial...And people do, including philosophers, because backwards ideas and a philosophy dedicated to preserving these ideas does not always vanish when it is clear that they no longer possess the same level of rational force.

When the emergence of a scientific terrain, or an earth-shaking development within such a terrain, alters reality and the way in which we see reality, it does not make it less true when, long after it has established its truth procedure, reactionary theorists and philosophers cling to opposing terrains that should have been annihilated. Nor is the labour of these thinkers autonomous from those truth procedures they wish to deny: the six-day creationist, for example, is forced to deny reality with the very tools that their opponents' terrain has placed at their disposal.

"The caesura affected by Marx has been more or less clearly acknowledged," writes Balibar; "it has even given rise to violent refutations and strenuous attempts at neutralization. But this has only caused it to haunt the totality of contemporary philosophical discourse all the more and to work on that discourse from within."[10] These "violent refutations" can be found in mainstream philosophy's attempt to code itself according to a canon that rejects the rupture "affected by Marx", and yet these denials happen within a context that cannot help but be haunted by the very fact of this rupture. Such canonical denials are merely attempts at damage control, a safe-guarding of the discipline from that which questions its autonomy, so that debate can continue without consciously accepting the very basis for this debate: class struggle and the social commitments behind all philosophical positions. Hence, the debates between those philosophies deemed worthy of canonization may be little more than evidence of a construction of a history of philosophy that is intended to remain free from Marxist contamination.

And yet the very fact that it conceives itself as possessing a history, not to mention a history of struggle, confirms the very fact it has been trying to deny—that Marxism necessitates the rearticulation of the entire practice of philosophy.

The class nature of philosophy?

Although the history of Marxism is replete with claims regarding philosophy's class nature, there has often been philosophical confusion over what this means. As discussed in the first chapter, various interpretations of the eleventh *Theses on Feuerbach* have produced this confusion which is why there is a tendency to dismiss philosophy altogether as a bourgeois practice, search for new philosophical foundations for the Marxist project, assume that philosophy is only properly philosophy if it can change the world, or fall back on the most orthodox definition of "Marxist philosophy" where *dialectical materialism* is the science that accompanies *historical materialism*.

First of all, while it is correct to recognize that philosophy can and has been a bourgeois practice, we should not dismiss it altogether as an idealist discipline. Such a dismissal is based on a rather narrow definition, if it even possesses a definition, of philosophy. The previous chapter on theoretical terrains, which generally puts philosophy in its place in relation to theory, should demonstrate, along with the claims made in the first chapter, that such a banal dismissal of philosophy concerns something else that goes by the name *philosophy*, whatever this something might be.

Secondly, to claim that a revolutionary project requires proper philosophical foundations again fails to understand the meaning of philosophy, attributing too much ontological importance to what is primarily a practice of intervention on what is already presented. Theoretical foundations are necessary, philosophy can perhaps reveal something about these theoretical foundations, but otherwise the unfolding terrain of Marxism forbids such a backwards movement into the grand system-building of past idealist philosophies. In this light, it is no wonder that the first claim, which judges all of philosophy to be arrogantly idealist, possesses some measure of strength.

Thirdly, the assumption that a properly radical philosophy is in itself concerned with changing the world, though rightly recognizing the fact that philosophers occupy class positions and should engage in class struggle, also attributes too much power to a practice that is intended to serve this very theory of revolution. Such a claim possesses a logic that is similar to the second claim. Philosophy by itself is not so grand that it can transform reality; if this was the case then, as aforementioned, all we would need for a significant social transformation would be a debate between radical philosophers and their status quo counterparts.

Finally, although the orthodox definition of "Marxist philosophy" is severely limited, it still might tell us something about the class nature of philosophy as long as we understand its limits and refuse to abide by its simplistic and formulaic scission. Most importantly, in its separation of *dialectical materialism* from *historical materialism* there is the germinal understanding of the given theoretical terrain (the "science" of historical materialism), and the role of philosophy in relation to this terrain—the logic with which the philosopher of Marxism is meant to work will be dialectical and materialist. Moreover, the orthodox explanations regarding this scission (made by Plekhanov, Stalin, etc.) names, albeit simply and sometimes dogmatically, the class nature of philosophy: whereas bourgeois and/or reactionary philosophers utilize "mechanical materialism" or "dialectical idealism" to make sense of the world, proletarian philosophers utilize dialectical materialism.

While I agree that dialectical materialism is an important methodology produced by the Marxist terrain (again I emphasize that philosophy is also and always conditioned by its fidelity to a given terrain), and is perhaps useful to understand in order to practise philosophy with a certain level of nuance, this may be a second-order question when it comes to philosophical praxis.[11] The problem of philosophical class commitments, though slightly illuminated by this now orthodox Marxist definition, spill beyond the boundaries of the formulaic claim that dialectical materialism is the philosophy of the oppressed and exploited. After all, it is possible to call oneself a dialectical materialist, and write books defending and defining dialectical materialism, and still be on the side of oppression and exploitation—history is filled with Marxist academics, intellectuals and organizations who collaborated with normative power structures regardless of how sophisticated their understanding of dialectical materialism was on paper. Although it is indeed correct to claim, on one level, that dialectical materialism is the philosophical method of the masses who make history, it does not fully illuminate the problem of political commitments that lurk behind every instance of philosophical practice.

Class philosophy

In *Anti-Duhring* Engels writes some rather interesting things about moral philosophy that might also tell us something, once wrenched from its particularity, about the class nature of philosophical practice. Although citing this passage might encourage a return to orthodoxy, I would hope that the reader is open-minded enough not to dismiss classical texts out of some uncritical obsession with contemporary academic fads. The point, here, is not to dogmatically rely on this passage as if it is theoretical "gospel" but instead to discover what the great revolutionary theorists of the past, regardless of their limitations, can teach us about theory and philosophy now.

In any case, writing in response to Eugen Duhring's assumption that socialism requires a proper ethical/moral philosophical system, Engels claims:

We therefore reject every attempt to impose on us any moral dogma whatsoever as an eternal, ultimate and for ever immutable ethical law on the pretext that the moral world, too, has its permanent principles which stand above history and the differences between nations. We maintain, on the contrary that all moral theories have been hitherto the product, in the last analysis, of the economic conditions of society obtaining at the time. And as society has hitherto moved in class antagonisms, morality has always been class morality; it has either justified the domination and the interests of the ruling class, or ever since the oppressed class became powerful enough, it has represented its indignation against this domination and the future interests of the oppressed. [...] But we have not yet passed beyond class morality. A really human morality which stands above class antagonisms and above any recollection of them becomes possible only at a stage of society which has not only overcome class antagonisms but has even forgotten them in practical life.[12]

Now if we replace the problematic of moral philosophy in particular with that of philosophy in general then we might have a useful framework for understanding the role of philosophy in relation to social context. There is no unconditioned philosophy that stands outside of social history; rather, philosophy is conditioned by history and the theoretical terrains—also the products of history—from which it emerges. We can thus argue that the normative practice of philosophy, which often treats itself as unconditioned, is in fact thoroughly conditioned, in the last instance, by ruling class hegemony; we can conversely claim that those philosophical interventions that admit conditioning and, upon this admission, attempt to intervene in a manner, however vaguely, that serves the oppressed, belong to a philosophical practice that is attempting to produce an alternate hegemony based on a different way of apprehending reality.[13]

Most importantly: "We have not yet passed beyond class *philosophy.*" Just as the ethicists must choose, or have the choice made for them, to place themselves in service to a social position so too is the philosopher forced to make a similar choice. In this sense, philosophy does not stand above the class contradictions that are foundational to a given theoretical terrain any more than theory itself stands above these contradictions; rather, a given practice of philosophy is mediated by "the conditions of society obtaining at the time" of its emergence. The apprehension of this mediation is primarily contained within a complex of theoretical terrains that produce philosophy only so that philosophy can be applied back on these terrains' mapping, just as the cartographer manifests in a particular geography so as to turn their attention upon the meaning of geography as a whole. To return us to the analogy with which this book opened, Sriduangkaew's character Ziyi, who appears to occupy an anterior position to the terrain in which she must make a political decision (that at first is presented as a purely logical and professional practice) based on her own implication in the terrain and yet the decision she makes forces the narrative's meaning.

In this context it is possible to appreciate Badiou's ontological project, the drawbacks of which I will discuss in another chapter. Grasping the fact that the practice of philosophy, rather than being foundational, is always conditioned, Badiou argued, in *Being and Event,* that mathematics *is* ontology. That is, rather than a philosophical system providing the foundations for any and every scientific theory, Badiou claimed that the theoretical terrain of mathematics was instead a condition (amongst others) *for* philosophy. And though I have argued that the deepest conditioning is the law of historical motion, it is still important to note that Badiou's counter-ontology is concerned with putting philosophy in its place, destabilizing its claim to unconditioned privilege. To riff on Meillassoux's comments about Badiou, but for an altogether different reason, although our project "is not the same as Badiou's, it is thanks to his singular project that we have been able to discover the means through which to extricate ourselves from the ontological conditions"[14] of the more antiquated and "noble" project of philosophy. Hence we must go further than Badiou, or at the very least mimic his reversal, and argue that the motion of history conditions philosophy.

Struggle and commitment

At this point it is necessary to discuss what I mean by "class struggle" and "class commitment", especially due to the way in which these terms are used by orthodox Marxism. Although I believe we still have much to learn from the tradition of classical Marxism that has ossified into various orthodoxies, and that to abandon this history altogether would be an abdication of thought, I do agree that orthodoxy by its very definition produces dogmatic expressions of concepts that should have a wider and more sophisticated application.

If I have used terms such as *political commitment, social embededness, historical positionality*—all of which may be more acceptable than the older concept of class commitment—I have done so for the sake of clarity and as ciphers for that which I take to be foundational, the problematic of class struggle. The reason I take this problematic to be foundational is because I consider it to be more coherent, though no less complex, than these other terms that by themselves are often quite confused.

To be clear, it is important that we do not mistake the concept of social class as, due to its orthodox interpretations, a downplaying of the myriad sites of social being that can and should be understood according to race, gender, sexuality, ability, etc. There is, after all, a way of treating class as its own particular identity that is most often reducible to a white and heterosexual man who works in an industrial factory: elsewhere I have referred to this treatment of class as *class essentialism* and I stand by that critique.[15] There is indeed "a tendency within Marxism that subordinates all other 'particular wrongs' experienced by others (such as those experienced by women or by the colonized) to the historico-teleological mission of the proletariat".[16] Since I ascribe to a Marxist trajectory that opposes this tendency, my understanding of social class as the basis for political commitment—as that which underlies all social positions—rejects this understanding of class while simultaneously refusing to treat class as an identity position that, through an intersectional analysis, stands alongside other identity positions. Rather, I argue that we should understand social class as the moment of intersection. As Butch Lee and Red Rover put it: "[i]n class society what is man-made is always disguised as the natural, the biological, or the Holy. What we think of as race or gender or nationality is class in drag."[17]

I do not want to lose myself in a tangent engaging with the definition of class, which is beyond the scope of this book, but I will say several things in this regard.[18] For the interest of brevity, I am going to assume my readers possess a general understanding of *class* and, based on this assumption, simply point out my conception of the bourgeois-proletariat relationship that defines modern capitalism is one that is co-determined by other sites of oppression. As Frantz Fanon once argued, in the context of settler-colonialism, "you are rich because you are white, you are white because you are rich".[19] Class formation and composition is co-determined by the concrete fact of other oppressions that exist in a given society even if, in the "lonely hour of the last instance that never arrives", the contradiction of economic class is theoretically primary: it may be far more difficult for a disabled and queer person of colour at the centres of capitalism, for instance, to become a member of the bourgeoisie but it is still possible, though the possibility possesses a far lower statistical assurance than if this individual was a straight, white, able-bodied, cis male. If and when an oppressed/marginalized individual succeeds in joining the first world ruling class, in defiance of the social barriers that make class mobility difficult for those who experience various oppressions, even though they will still face the material facticity of their particular oppressions they will also possess the ability to mitigate these other oppressions in comparison to their proletarian counterparts.

We must note, however, that such mitigation is most often partial, particularly in societies where concrete histories of oppression have erected oppressive class boundaries, producing various subject positions. For example, in a white supremacist society not only is the ruling class composition predominantly white, the minority bourgeois individuals who are not white will still experience the structural barriers of oppression which possess a history of policing the foundational structure of class. Hence, in a white supremacist settler society such as the US, class was (and is) structured in a very racialized manner so that one cannot make sense of social class without taking racism into account. In the early days of developing US capitalism, black slaves, being property, were by definition excluded from the possibility of class mobility, the supposed hallmark of capitalism, and indigenous people were slated for extermination and marginalization. When slavery ended multiple laws were enacted to defend the white hegemony of class society and this structuring of class persists in some sense, despite various revolutionary challenges, to this day. All outliers were precisely that—outliers—and, like the "rags to riches" mythologies used to justify the nobility of capitalism, these exceptions are often used to obscure the racist class structure. "Class structure," writes Erik Olin Wright, "imposes limits on class formation, class consciousness and class struggle."[20] When the class structure of a given society is partially structured according to a racist ethos, then secondary rules about the formation of bourgeois and proletariat (i.e. how one gets to belong to what class) persist and also affect our conscious understanding of class and how class struggle is carried out.

The Obamas, for example, were clearly and unapologetically representatives of the bourgeois-imperialist order and yet they still experienced the racism generated by a white supremacist settler society. While it would be bizarre to assume that their experience of racism was the same as what was experienced by individuals in a poor black community in Ferguson, it would also be odd to claim that they were unaffected by racism altogether. Even still, in the last instance it is their class position that matters; such a position allowed the Obama presidency to align itself with the white supremacist settler-capitalism that over-determines the class structure of the US. It is no accident that Barack Obama refused to defend the Black Lives Matter movement, the multiple race rebellions that erupted at the end of his presidency, and went so far as to legitimate racist police violence by supporting "Blue Lives Matter" legislation. The racist structuring of the US class contradiction, despite nearly 8 years of "post-race" denial, is again revealing its intractability with the return of the repressed in the form of resurgent fascism, symptomized by Donald Trump's election.

Other sites of oppression can be similarly understood through the moment of intersection that is class structure (because class is the base structure of a social formation, rather than a particular identity, since it contains multiple and conflicting identities) although, depending on the society in question, the way in which they affect and are affected by social class will vary.

In any case, since I discuss this problematic elsewhere, I will move on. Let us simply accept that there is such a thing as class struggle, however broadly we may wish to define it, that is at the same time a struggle that can and must account for sites of marginalization and oppression that some may erroneously assume have nothing to do with social class. Let us also assume that these struggles between the oppressed and their oppressors, and the co-determined struggle between the exploited and their exploiters, influence the way in which people comprehend the world in which they live, thus generating different commitments.

While I do not believe it is the case that this production of class commitment completely determines the human subject (we are not so passively *subjected* that we cannot think outside of the social position we occupy so as to align ourselves with the oppressed/exploited) we should recognize that social being significantly affects social consciousness. Our commitment, and thus the ethics and side of the social struggle(s) we choose to endorse, is severely conditioned by our social position. The above reference to Wright's analysis of social class should make this point clear: the particular class structure of a given society will delimit class formation, consciousness, and even struggle—all the elements that comprise one's social position.

What does this mean for the practice of philosophy? Only that, since it is practised by people who are socially embedded and historically positioned, such practice is always conditioned by history, drenched in the residue of class commitment and struggle. As Etienne Balibar reminds us: "Philosophy is not an autonomous activity, but one determined by the position it occupies in the field of social conflicts and, in particular, in that of the class struggle."[21]

Tangent: cartographic imperialism

I want to briefly return to the metaphor of cartography I employed in the previous chapter and elaborate on my rushed thoughts about its underlying tension, a tension that might shed some light on the conflicted practice of philosophy. As aforementioned, the mapping of geographic terrains possesses a history that is complicit with imperial power: colonizers and neo-colonizers have written and rewritten the landscape of the globe, parcelling out nation-states to themselves and their vassals. "They transform the geography into their vision of what the geography should be," Edward Said said in a discussion with Mona Hatoum: "They rename it, they efface its history. So the drawing and redrawing of maps is the endless transformation not only of the land but also of the possession of the land."[22] In Antti-Jussi Annila's film *Sauna* (2008), which follows a group of state-sanctioned map-makers tasked to redraw national borders without any care for the people being demarcated, the opening credits are a blank parchment upon which blood streams to ink out the contours of national power.

To reemphasize what I asserted in the second chapter, my choice of this analogy is thus meant to signal the complicity that literal map-making has with the ravages of Empire as well as the possibility of a counter-practice. Philosophy, since it is not outside of class struggle, can also be complicit with an oppressive state of affairs; the philosopher can thus be akin to an imperial cartographer, an agent who seeks to demarcate meaning that will justify a predatory terrain and/or extend the logic of its boundaries. The ruling class promotes its own philosophers to justify its ruling ideas, after all, and philosophy departments are filled with bourgeois ideologues. When the alt-right ideologue Richard Spencer was punched in the face, to use a rather pithy example, supposedly "objective" moral philosophers were asked by *Newsweek* to judge whether or not this single act of anti-fascist violence was ethical. Most of these philosophers said *no* and thus demonstrated the fact that a political decision is always prior to the philosophical intervention: the lines they drew were complicit with the boundaries of liberal capitalism.[23] But a philosopher in the service of an anti-fascist ideology would provide a different ethical interpretation.

To reemphasize, just as the history of cartography cannot escape its complicity with the imperial mutilation of the globe, there is also the fact that alternate boundaries have been drawn, and rebel terrains have been punched out of the world's fabric, by revolutionary and anti-colonial movements. The multiple processes of decolonization that erupted in the 1950s led to successive redrawings of boundaries determined by the world-shaking rebellions of defiant subaltern nations. Some of these redrawings were assimilated into the nexus of imperial power, some were rejected altogether, some are still yet to be accomplished. Cutting up the terrain of colonial power with new cartographies is the business of revolutionary movements. Imagine, if you will, the possibility of the US or Canada being demarcated by the boundary lines of multiple oppressed nations: such a cartography, the angry shadow of its imperial double, would carve out another world.

Hence philosophy as an exercise of demarcation confronts us with a choice: side with the cartographic operations of the state of affairs and the preservation of business as usual, or take its place alongside those who seek to draw new lines, explore new terrains of meaning, and efface the boundaries of ruling class ideology.

Whose philosophy and for whom?

Accepting the axiom that every theoretical terrain and philosophical intervention is conditioned by history and thus conditioned by class struggle may at first appear to be a banal presupposition. In some ways this assumption is correct; any fact of reality is banal insofar as it is just something that *is* and is perhaps no more profound than the assertion that we need water to live. Underneath this banality, however, is an important insight that is connected to questions of meaning and interpretation, particularly what it means to apprehend a theoretical terrain and engage with its unfolding.

Questions about political commitments that condition a given terrain, as well as condition the practice of philosophy, are questions that, if ignored, allow the conditioned to pass as unconditioned and thus result in a failure of thought. The fact of the matter is that the commitments behind a terrain's particular development, as well as philosophers' manner(s) of engagement, are concerned with the establishment of meaning.

If the presuppositions that lead to such an establishment are left interrogated, or if the interrogators themselves are unconscious of their commitments, then we may find ourselves at a dead-end of bad faith where common sense ideology is reified. Hence, returning to Marx's *Theses on Feuerbach*, "the educator must be educated". Thus, questions of commitment are necessary for the forcing of meaning; we abandon them at the peril of dismissing a given terrain's importance.

Take, for example, Mao's dictum regarding the terrain of literature and art that can be distilled into the slogan: *whose art and for whom?* Asking such a question may, at first glance, seem crude since some artists and theorists might desire an autonomous unfolding of art and aesthetic theory according to its own logic (a position that can be simplified under the cliché "art for art's sake") due to the suspicion of nefarious political intervention. And yet, if we do not ask about the political commitments underlying artistic production we risk reifying art, transforming it into a self-unfolding process that takes place outside of human practice. Moreover, such a question forces us to consider successive questions of artistic production that in turn produce different artistic practices, all of which lead to the terrain's development. Are there provinces of fascist art and socialist art within the artistic terrain, why should we assume that there are not, and how do we understand the boundaries that demarcate such provinces? The meaning behind a specific artistic movement, itself a (sub)terrain with its own truth procedure, can only be grasped by a critical intervention that is also conditioned by one's social conditioning; to assume otherwise is to treat this terrain as meaningless since it just *is* and, by existing beyond that which can force meaning, is thus tantamount to a barren terrain. Think, here, of the disjuncture between futurism and constructivism: the former was an aesthetic expression of political reaction, with Marinetti merging the futurist movement with the Italian Fascist Party; the latter expressed the aesthetics of the Bolshevik Revolution, with Mayakovsky's state funeral rivalling that of Lenin's. Clarifying the meaning of such artistic moments is the business of philosophy and, likewise, tells us something about philosophy.

All philosophies that have been critical in more than name have recognized the importance of grounding their practice in these *whose and for whom* questions: we only need to examine the philosophical branch of epistemology for evidence of this fact. On the one hand there are those epistemologies that attempt to make sense of knowledge without examining how knowledge is conditioned by social class and ideological commitment, assuming the knower and the known can be treated in an abstract manner (unconditioned and objective) and that this is the height of critical investigation. On the other hand there are those critical epistemologies that are deeply suspicious of an unconditioned knower and refuse to accept that it is fallacious to connect the knower's circumstances to what the knower claims can be known despite the worries of the *circumstantial ad hominem* fallacy. In this critical tradition that attempts to excavate the very grounds upon which knowledge is constructed, we discover feminist epistemologists such as Lorraine Code echoing Mao's dictum by grounding their investigation in the question *whose knowledge and for whom?*

Although the practice of philosophy in general concerns the forcing of meaning so as to make sense of the world, such a practice will fall short of its aims if it assumes that the very act of making sense emerges from a position unconditioned by conflicting social classes. A meaning will be forced, a "making sense" will be established, but it will lurk only on a given terrain's surface content to call its bad faith objectivity "critical thinking" when, in actual fact, it is doing little more than reifying normative relations of power. Here we should be reminded of Descartes, whose apparently radical approach to the epistemological project became the normalization of the bourgeois, male subject. Or Rawls whose "first position" and "veil of ignorance" theories of justice were veiled capitalist social relations that took, without reflection, the free market as the original position. Or even Nietzsche, the bad conscience of these more "sober-minded" philosophical practices, whose totalizing critique of morality was conditioned by the morality of the bourgeois individual.

Hence, a terrain's meaning will become fully coherent if and only if we begin our engagement with an understanding of class commitment—the logic behind historical development. A given theory's meaning, and the philosophical attempt to force this meaning, becomes more apparent, coherent, and indeed meaningful when grasped according to its historical conditioning. And though it is correct to recognize that this axiom of historical conditioning is also part of a theoretical terrain that cannot escape its own premises, it is also correct to respond that, by being in the world, we cannot escape the world and thus, however which way we want an underlying theory to make sense of this fact, cannot flee from history and society.

In the end the philosopher must turn this question of commitment upon the practice of philosophy itself: *whose philosophy and for whom?*

Notes

1. Althusser, *Philosophy and the Spontaneous Philosophy of the Scientists*, 10-11.

2. Carole Condé and Karl Beveridge's installation at the Art Gallery of Ontario (AGO), *It's Still Privileged Art* (1975) is a paradigm example of this kind of confrontation. When they were signed for the AGO installation they were still working under the auspices of a seemingly apolitical formalism. In the period between their signing and the actual installation, however, they were politicized and thus ended up producing a show that challenged the authority of the art institution that

pretended to be above politics. They filled the respectable space with slogans ("art must become responsible for its politics"), challenged the institutional authority with every piece, and produced a programme booklet that was inspired by the Chinese Cultural Revolution. A wealthy sponsor withdrew his name from the museum and Condé and Beveridge were blacklisted from an institution that pretended to be above politics.

3. Yami, 102.

4. Code, *Rhetorical Spaces*, 33.

5. Marx, *Grundrisse*, 111.

6. Benjamin, 222.

7. Ibid., 224.

8. As well as a rejection of human nature that, though claiming to be materialist because of the ways in which "human nature" was often defined by appeals to a mystical essence (hence Sartre's complaint about the concept of human essence), is in fact idealist in its rejection of biological science proves there is a material human nature. In *Gramsci, Materialism, and Philosophy*, Morera makes a compelling argument that a conception of human nature, due to scientific investigation, is necessarily materialist and all attempts to deny it, even when they pretend to be materialist, are in fact a denial of materialism.

9. Althusser, *On the Reproduction of Capitalism*, 11.

10. Balibar, *The Philosophy of Marx*, 4-5.

11. One of my past projects, *Torsion and Tension*, was a philosophical intervention upon the concept of "dialectical materialism". I eventually abandoned the project because I eventually became convinced that it was too opaque and unwieldy, posting its final draft chapters (which I was not satisfied with) on my blog. My experience with that project, though, convinced me of a comment Marx made to Engels about *Capital*'s relationship with the *Grundrisse*: that the

"scaffolding" of dialectical logic in the latter needed to be less apparent when he moved on to write the former.

12. Engels, *Anti-Duhring*, 87-88.

13. I have intentionally avoided the term *counter-hegemony* since I feel that without qualification it has become conceptually loaded, in the past 3 or 4 decades, so as to produce a certain level of confusion. That is, there is a somewhat bland schematization of Gramsci's concept of hegemony that formalizes "hegemony" as the problem of normative power and "counter-hegemony" as the solution. The truth, however, is that Gramsci treated "hegemony" as a bare concept and simply argued that, since capitalism currently possessed hegemony, part of a revolutionary movement's business was to replace capitalist hegemony with socialist hegemony. Thus, a counter-hegemonic movement is one that is simply seeking to replace one hegemony with another, that seeks to make its values "common sense". Obviously, counter-hegemonic movements can also be reactionary.

14. Meillassoux, 103.

15. See, for example, Moufawad-Paul, *The Communist Necessity*, 78-79; Moufawad-Paul, *Continuity and Rupture*, 123-127.

16. Shaw, 46.

17. Lee and Rover, 7.

18. I have examined this elsewhere, such as in *Continuity and Rupture* (112-127), and plan to return to this problematic in the future.

19. Fanon, *The Wretched of the Earth*, 40.

20. Wright, *Classes*, 27.

21. Balibar, 4.

22. Quoted in Hatoum, 39. We should note, here, that Hatoum's work that concerns maps and mapping aptly demonstrates the ways in which artists politically intervene, drawing their own demarcations, on the order of the real. Her most iconic example of an artistic politicization of the map is

Present Tense (1996), an installation consisting of thousands of blocks of olive oil soap upon which the topography of Palestine is traced with glass beads. Here we have the map of the nation, represented as indigenous through the choice of olive oil and traditional beads, mutilated into flesh like slabs by colonial bantustanization. We are thus presented with two topographies, locked in an antagonistic colonial contradiction: the one represented by the beads and the olive oil, the indigenous nation that Palestinians yearn for; the one represented by thousands of pieces, the colonial occupation that draws innumerable borders (both on the land and in every aspect of existence) across the colonized nation.

23. Zach Schonfeld, "Is it okay to punch a Nazi in the Face? Leading Ethicists Weigh In: 'No'" (http://www.newsweek. com/richard-spencer-punch-nazi-ethicists-547277)

Chapter Four

philosophy and clarity

Philosophy...is the urge to be at home everywhere.
Georg Lukács, The Theory of the Novel

Plato is known for arguing that the poets should be banned from his ideal republic. The truth, however, is that he only suggested that a certain type of poetry should be banned and that poetic excess should be submitted to state sanctions. His sanctions against poetry, though, are presumed to be an attack on artistic freedom. While it is indeed the case that Plato assaults artistic freedom, it is also the case that we are dealing with a political moment that predates liberal conceptions of free expression. Hence, we should treat Plato's explicit decision for censoring poetry according to its actual logic. The most apparent reason for controlling poetry, and the one often lamented by modern interlocutors, is because it is deceitful and thus misleads us from a correct apprehension of the truth. For the contemporary reader, who immediately thinks of the history of poetry and art to date, Plato appears to be claiming that metaphor and analogy—artistic form in itself—has no basis in a just state of affairs: millennia before Orwell's "Big Brother" Plato is advocating censorship for the sake of censorship.

But Plato is not talking about the poet of the modern world, or about what poetry has become thousands of years since ancient Athens. Once again we are stuck with that problem of names and concepts: *poetry* and *the poets* mean something conceptually different in Plato's time compared to ours. The poet in the ancient Greek world was someone who believed themselves to be divinely inspired, a mouthpiece of the mystic order; poetry was religious text and the poems known to Plato were intended to be divine representations of reality that described lightening as the business of Zeus, rainbows as messages written by the gods, and creation as a contradictory and obscure process of mystic metaphor.

The emergence of early Greek philosophy before Plato was an emergence in defiance of the poetic order. The so-called "pre-Socratics", militants of the Ionian Enlightenment, were attempting to demystify the world by stealing the purchase of reality from the esoteric claims of poetic inspiration. That is, philosophy in that region of the world and time was defined primarily by the ethos of demystification: to make reality clear, to remove the obscure haze of the Homers and Hesiods, to investigate, clarify, and demarcate. In reaction to philosophy, the order of the poets sentenced Socrates to death. Thus, with all this in mind, Plato's ban on a certain order of poetry was not primarily a ban on artistic freedom because it was not concerned with modern conceptualizations of poetry. Rather, Plato was proposing a philosophical order of politics: if we could found a just system based on demystification then that which opposes clarification—that which reasserts the lie of a mystic order— must necessarily be rejected. While it is indeed the case that Plato's philosophical-political order is not a desirable state of affairs, we should at least recognize that its ban on poetry (as poetry was defined in Plato's time) was necessarily motivated by the meaning of philosophy itself. Philosophical practice has always opposed mystification; it is not the poetry of the ancients.

Hence, in light of my earlier claim regarding the interpretive aspect of philosophy, in this chapter I want to examine philosophy as that practice that, to use Wittgenstein's definition mentioned earlier, is the "logical clarification of thought"— forcing meaning, demanding decision, explaining the commitments behind particular theoretical assumptions, casting the mystifier out of an imaginary philosophical republic.[1] Here, *clarity* does not mean *simplification*: while it may be the case that the reduction of complex concepts and issues to an easily understandable summary may make some phenomena clear, it is also the case that such a reduction obscures the fact that it is the complexity itself that needs to be clear. Take, for example, the reduction of the complex issue of oppression's relationship to exploitation to the simplistic and summary claim that sexism, racism, homophobia, ableism, etc. is nothing more than a tactic to divide an otherwise united exploited proletariat. Such a simplification clarifies nothing; it actually obscures the concrete fact of oppression behind a simplistic platitude that, while on the surface level true (the proletariat *is* divided by multiple oppressions), actually explains nothing (why is it so prone to division in the first place, through what conspiratorial method is such division accomplished) and thus cannot make the phenomena it seeks to simplify clear in any sense of the term.

To clarify, therefore, is not necessarily to simplify; it is to align oneself with the most concrete explanation of a concrete phenomenon even if this explanation, at first glance, defies simplicity. The more complex the phenomena, the more amphibological the terrain in which philosophy intervenes, the more complex the philosophical intervention. In this chapter, in a recursive attempt to clarify the philosophical task of forcing clarity, I will focus on the ways in which philosophy can provide clarity and how such a clarity, following the Marxist rupture, also concerns demystification and thus the limits of purely speculative philosophy.

Although such an approach to philosophy possesses its own dangers, where one either assimilates their self to the status quo or betrays the radicality of this philosophical practice, in many ways it is unavoidable since we are often forced into a spontaneous practice of philosophy when we reach those theoretical junctures that require the supervention of interpretation. In the second proposition of the first chapter I argued that "[p]hilosophy is that which takes problems encountered in reality...as objects of interpretations and reflection". We encounter such problems as a matter of course simply by thinking, and we may often find ourselves in the realm of philosophy without realizing that this is the case. As Gramsci understood, everyone at some point in their life is a philosopher. The quality of our philosophical practice, however, can be gauged by the clarity it produces— whether or not it leads us to an interpretation where a choice in thought is clear, whether or not it can force decision. Hence, there are times when we are engaging in the practice of philosophy unconsciously, imagining we are producing theory (and conversely the opposite is the case where philosophers imagine they are theorists, even scientists and mathematicians), and such a spontaneous practice rarely succeeds in producing clarity. If we are to force clarity—if we are to force a decision in thought—then we must do so in a conscious manner, aware of the precise practice in which we are engaged.

Logically clarifying thought

The clarity that philosophical intervention can provide to a given theoretical terrain is a clarity that is often provided when we are faced with a choice between competing terrains and/ or provinces. In the act of drawing demarcating lines we are occasionally led to call into question one or more theoretical regions. In comparing these often contradictory regions, each with their own regime of truth, the role of philosophy is, as Badiou has noted, to force a choice.

As discussed in the first chapter, it is not the business of a particular theory to explain the meaning of its truth value as compared to competing theoretical geographies; the proof of its truth procedure is supposed to be contained within the theory itself, an operational description of what *is* or what *is not*. The General and Special Theories of Relativity, for example, are truth claims that do not seek to explain, by themselves, why they provide a more meaningful interpretation of phenomena than the Newtonian paradigm; they simply provide proofs of their veracity according to a rarified internal logic that is meant to account for the phenomena in question. Explaining the difference in meaning between different theories, what these differences mean, and why one should side with one over another is the business of philosophy. Which is why scientists often become spontaneous philosophers when they realize the implication of theory and thus desire to explain the implied meaning.

Upon encountering competing theoretical trajectories in a larger terrain, however, the practice of philosophy discovers another problem: how can it force a choice, as well as providing clarity for this choice, between these different regions of theory? In other words, upon what grounds can and should the would-be philosopher force a choice of the theory of the Big Bang, for example (and to pick a debate that most physicists consider solved), over the theory of the Constant Continuum? The answer is simultaneously simple and complex: by the logic of the larger theoretical terrain in which this forcing of choice occurs. Simple because it appears obvious that a theory regarding a question in the terrain of physics should accord to the overall logic of the terrain of physics as it has developed to this point; complex because it is often quite difficult to demonstrate—and herein lies the struggle of philosophy—why one theory rather than another better accords to this logic.

In retrospect the forcing of the theory of the Big Bang makes sense since it provides a better explanatory account of physical phenomena than the theory of the Constant Continuum, but we only know this in retrospect. Part of the struggle in thought, whether it was the spontaneous philosophy of the scientists or an intentional philosophy of science, was in establishing the veracity of the Big Bang theory over that of the Constant Continuum by providing the kind of clarity that was meant to prove that the former could provide a better account, according to the overall terrain of physics, of what was meant to be explained. In attempting to provide this clarity those philosophers of science who sided with what we now accept as the correct theory were forced to combat all of the muddled but still philosophical mappings that treated the theory of the Big Bang in a mystified manner.

Philosophy, then, remains in its proper place if the choice it attempts to force within a given region accords with the overall logic of this region's terrain. To argue that philosophy is "the logical clarification of thought" should mean that any clarification of thought proceeds in a manner where the forcing of truth is not cosmetic, nor is simply an assumption put forward like a theoretical axiom, but is something that is wed to the overall logic of a given terrain. There are innumerable bad faith interventions that attempt to make sense of a specific scientific terrain according to the logic of aesthetics, or vice versa, and these philosophical projects force nothing but confusion. The progenitors of what is now deemed "analytic philosophy" may have had good reason, however limited this reason became in the end, to confine philosophy to the rules of formal logic: if philosophy could be no more than an intervention upon various theoretical terrains so as to force meaning, then it was perhaps most useful to reduce this intervention to rules of logical consistency intended to operationalize meaning

Clarity and competing regions

But even before we ask questions about competing regions/ provinces/fields within a specific theoretical terrain, we often need to draw lines between larger terrains that are competing for ascendancy in thought on the same problematic. Philosophers tend to favour some terrains over others, and are most often obsessed with rejecting entire bodies of theory so as to force an acceptance of the theory or theories they believe are the most worthwhile. This concern is behind the entire project of early modern philosophy that was militantly invested, irregardless of multiple mistakes and confusions, in championing the scientific terrains over the religious terrains when it came to making sense of human existence. The latter terrains were treated as mystified, tied to decaying feudal orders, whereas the former terrains became the locus of philosophical struggle—superior in that they possessed the kind of rational, explanatory depth that religious theory lacked. And though it is true that this championing sometimes led to an uncritical embrace of crude empiricism and positivist materialism, we need to appreciate the motivation behind this embattled intervention.

Thus, the reason why it is necessary to recognize that scientific terrains are the most important theoretical terrains is because of the historical importance of demystification. No other type of theoretical terrain provides the same level of explanatory depth, the type of truth procedure that can demystify phenomena by establishing concrete meaning. Philosophy thus becomes incoherent when it is dislocated from this concern and, in its refusal to name and demarcate scientific terrains, remystifies itself. None of this is to say that philosophy should not be critical of a scientific terrain—that it should not attempt to call into question the claims of would-be sciences and scientists— but only that its rejection of scientific terrains altogether may produce a moment of *anti-philosophy*, what Badiou has classified as sophistry.

On the whole, however, philosophy has been historically entangled with scientific terrains—so much concerned that at points it has attempted to conflate itself with science (and thus liquidate itself in the theoretical terrain), or pretend that it can provide science with its foundations (and thus presume it possesses a truth procedure that pre-conditions scientific truth). Despite these erroneous positions, the main reason why philosophy is often obsessed with scientific terrains is because these terrains concretely operationalize truth procedures in a way that other terrains cannot. Scientific theories of electricity, unlike religious and/or occult theories, actually lead to the production of energy and light—they are thus philosophically significant because they are *meaningful* in a way that some theory of magical "witch light" can never be: I can flip a switch, or plug an appliance into the wall, and never have to worry about prayers and/or magical incantations.

Althusser's claim that "the foundation of an important new science has always more or less overturned and renewed existing philosophy"[2] is worthy of some reflection since it helps explain what I mean by philosophy's relationship to scientific terrains. After all, since philosophy has always become confused, altered, and regenerated by ruptural moments in a given scientific terrain, it has also developed as a discipline because of this type of theoretical terrain. Following Althusser, we can argue that there would be no Plato or Aristotle without prior developments in the field of mathematics, no Descartes without Galileo, no Kant without Newton.[3]

Any philosophical investigation into non-scientific terrains is done in a manner that has been intimately affected by a given philosophy's anterior instance—where it was stamped by the science that overturned and renewed its character. Thus, when a philosopher chooses to intervene on a terrain that is non-scientific, they do so with a philosophy already socialized by those scientific geographies philosophy also intends to map—even if the intention is to reject the basis of this marking altogether.

Hence philosophy possesses the strange characteristic of doubling back upon itself, of being able to turn its attention upon those terrains which make it possible: even if it is "overturned and renewed" by scientific developments, philosophy retains the ability to either force or call into question the meaning of that which provided its anterior point. Even those philosophical tendencies that are primarily concerned with calling scientific terrains into question are still indelibly marked by these terrains and would not have been possible without the object of their critique: would Foucault's project, for example, make any sense without the tools it inherited from the object of its critique? After all, Foucault ended his totalizing critique by returning to the very question that he initially found suspicious, the question philosophy inherited from the "new sciences" of early modernity that was also asked by Kant: *what is enlightenment?*

Thus, if philosophy is to be conscious of its own practice it needs to be aware of that which makes it possible even if it is turning its attention back upon the basis of its own possibility. Such an awareness—which puts philosophy in its place while at the same time permitting the critical autonomy to force meaning—is what allows a rigorous mapping, the drawing of lines between competing terrains. Marked by the sciences, philosophy is not only armed with the ability to use the logic of scientific truth procedures upon other terrains, it can also use this same logic upon scientific terrains themselves. In this sense, and again despite its problems, analytic philosophy is marked by the tendency to utilize the logical language of consistency and clarity—formal logic, validity and soundness, etc.—in order to judge the terrains upon which it intervenes.

On Althusser (1) — philosophy as practice

In order to provide a deeper meaning to the concept of clarity, I want to discuss my decision to locate the origin of a conscious philosophical practice in the Althusserian project. Such a discussion will teach us something about the practice of philosophy in clarifying thought. Although that project was doomed to encounter the limitations of that period's already waning Marxism-Leninism—the onslaught of a revisionism that was apprehended but never fully understood, and therefore all of the philosophical problems that could not be solved by recourse to a terrain that had reached its historical boundaries—the questions it posed, and the positions it staked out, are still the concern of any philosophy that dares to map the social and historical. The shadow it casts is immense; the philosophical problematic Althusser and his students enunciated continues to resonate with social philosophers and theorists who have dared to speak of radical critique and practice since 1968, even those who attempted to overstep this supposed "structuralism". And then there are the former students of Althusser, such as Alain Badiou and Jacques Rancière, who are still approaching philosophy according to Althusser's problematic even when they are critical of the routes taken by their late teacher.

It is my contention that what was important about this project, and what all post-Althusserian radical philosophies ignore at their peril, was not its historical provincialism that we now understand as "properly Althusserian"—that is, the rejection of the human subject, the concept of ideological state apparatuses, the epistemological break between the "young" and "mature" Marx, overdetermination. These were conceptual symptoms of a deeper project that, by its very nature, produced multiple and sometimes contradictory sites of investigation. Rather, the importance of Althusser's project is that: i) it was primarily a philosophical project, which was often misunderstand and, because of this, ii) it sought to put philosophy in its place in relation to theory and thus make sense of how science, particularly the self-proclaimed "science of history", related to the practice of philosophy. Simply put: to generally grasp philosophy as a concrete practice and to particularly grasp philosophy as a potentially militant practice. Therefore, it is no accident that the final coherent works Althusser wrote, especially those published posthumously, centre the problematic of philosophical meaning. For example, *On the Reproduction of Capitalism*, from which the infamous "ISA" essay was adapted and that was only published in total in 2014, begins with a chapter entitled "what is philosophy?"—a strange point of departure, one might imagine, for a book that at first glance seems to concern political economy. *Philosophy for Non-Philosophers* was also published in 2014 (though it would not receive an English translation until 2017) thus indicating, with his last substantial and systematic book, that Althusser's entire body of work could be unified in a concern for the meaning of philosophy in general and militant philosophical practice in particular.

In the conclusion of *Philosophy for Non-Philosophers* Althusser claimed, "to become a philosopher, and the equal of professional philosophers...one has to learn philosophy in practice, in the different practices and, above all, in the practice of class struggle".[4] The immediate corollary of such a claim, based on everything we have discussed, is to treat philosophy as a tool for demystifying the theoretical landscape so as to demarcate the terrains of ideology from the terrains of science. After all, following the above passage, Althusser adds: "*a philosopher is a man* [or woman or person] *who fights in theory*".[5]

That is to say, philosophy's role as a *practice of clarity* will mean for the philosophy of Marxism not only the practice of demystification but a practice done in the service of the oppressed and exploited. It is not enough to produce clarity; we must also produce a clarity wrenched from all forms of mystification that would seek to lock us back in the realm of ruling class ideology. Such production begins by recognizing that philosophy is part of class war, that philosophical practice is a "battlefield" especially when its bourgeois adherents proclaim otherwise. The philosophy of Marxism—the philosophy that *belongs* to Marxism—must be consciously placed in the service of class struggle as a weapon: to demystify, clarify, and unify theory, to struggle against aspects of theoretical terrains that are still hampered by mystic and anti-materialist thinking, and to even go so far as to demarcate itself from that philosophy that seeks to return us to the most abstract and anti-materialist forms of ontological speculation. After all, according to Althusser, this is what philosophy has been for the various strata of the ruling class: a weapon for the consolidation of its hegemony. "If every philosophy unfolds on class theoretical bases and unifies the existing ideological elements as the dominant ideology, for the dominant class's benefit," he writes, "it is easy to see why philosophy produces not knowledge, but only a weapon in the fight. A weapon is a weapon: it produces nothing but the power of victory."[6]

Thus, Althusser located the practice of militant philosophy in relation to the scientific terrain of historical materialism—that terrain which was concerned, first and foremost, with demystifying the world—and was thus forced to examine the transformation this terrain demanded for the practice of philosophy. Such a location, and the questions it engendered, would form the obsession of the *Cahiers pour l'Analyse* journal whose contributors would include Badiou, Miller, Leclaire, Foucault, Derrida, Regnault, Irigaray, Canguilhem, and others. Innumerable radical tendencies were launched by the Althusserian project, some of which travelled far beyond its concrete basis, and yet the questions it posed about the relationship of philosophy to theory, particularly to science and the science of history, still demand investigation.

Now that we are in the twenty-first century we have endured a long march through innumerable denunciations and dismissals of Althusser's root project—from Foucault's dismissal of Marxism's "totalizing" claim to *science*, to Deleuze and Guattari's theoretical eclecticism, to Baudrillard's nihilism, to Rancière's rejection of Althusser's "philosophy of order", to those other Marxist rejections of Althusser (either from E.P. Thompson or Trotskyist-influenced Marxist theory) that betrayed a poor understanding of his project, and finally to the capitalist "end of history" dogma. In this context, it may seem odd to demand a return to Althusser's problematic. And yet the groundwork of this project, which sought to make sense of a radical philosophical practice by grounding it according to "revolutionary science", is even more evocative now than it was in the past. Not those cosmetic aspects of Althusser that were mistaken as the core of his thought (the epistemic rupture, structuralism and anti-humanism, state apparatuses and interpellation) but the desire to conceptualize philosophy's relationship to class struggle, the attempt to demystify the practice of philosophy itself. After movementist strategies of revolt have failed to produce anything that can challenge the current state of affairs Althusser's philosophical clarity regarding science and ideology is again salient. As Peter Hallward writes in his introduction to the first edited volume of the *Cahiers pour l'Analyse* journal, after noting that Badiou has remained "faithful" to the spirit of Althusser's project:

> No doubt it is too early to say, towards the end of a tumultuous 2011, that the question of revolutionary change has returned to a prominent place in the philosophical agenda. But after decades dominated by the myriad forms of a backlash against radical politics (liberalism, deconstruction, "ethics", historicism, cynicism...), many younger thinkers and activists are at least more receptive now to the basic problem that "theoretical training" was meant to solve in the 1960s.[7]

In any case, what we find in the Althusserian project, regardless of its limitations, is a basic understanding of the division between theory and philosophy, particularly science or revolutionary science and philosophical practice, that provides clarity and a concrete grounding of philosophical practice that is simultaneously understood as a weapon of class struggle. While it may be correct to treat the entire structuralist project that Althusser helped bring into being as flawed, to simply declare along with Rancière that "[t]he great Althusserian project of struggle of science against ideology clearly turned out to be a struggle against the potential strength of mass revolt"[8] is a gross misunderstanding. For while we must recognize that Althusser eventually aligned himself with a conservative Marxism incapable of understanding that, as Mao tells us, "it is right to rebel" even if this rebellion is not guided by revolutionary science, it is also a fact that "it is better to make revolution". The May 1968 revolt, which Rancière had in mind, does not force "us to measure the gap between the actual history of social movements and the conceptual system inherited from Marx"[9] but, rather, confirms the necessity of understanding the relationship between science and philosophy.

To be clear, the May 1968 revolt in Paris followed precisely the course prescribed by a scientific assessment of spontaneity: it was barely an echo of the Commune and Althusser's failure to side with history's rebels in this case, especially when his students *were* siding with these rebels, neither helped nor hindered the rebellion. Indeed, any philosophical intervention, even one as grand as Althusser's, is incapable by itself of exerting such influence upon mass movements—that is at least one point we can glean from the Althusserian project and its rigorous embrace of theoretical training—but only intervenes in the realm of thought. There are times when such interventions fail to produce clarity.

On Althusser (2) — slippages between theory and philosophy

Any of the symptomatic "errors" made by Althusser are at least guided by the rigorous understanding of the role of philosophy and an attempt, based on this understanding, to force meaning upon and to explain a terrain that was treated as scientific. Althusser's contemporary relevance is in his work as a philosopher; where his project appears most open to critique— especially in its successive post-structuralist articulations—is at those moments where it slips into theory. As discussed above, the work from which one of his most famous essays, "Ideology and

Ideological State Apparatuses", was derived, *On the Reproduction of Capitalism*, begins with the question "what is philosophy?" and alerts us to the fact that he was not producing Marxist theory but, rather, taking the Marxist terrain (the "science" of historical materialism) as already pre-given as well as one filled with multiple confusions on the part of political economists who were trying to make sense of the questions raised, at that time, by the science.

As with any science there are competing trajectories; Althusser's project was simply to intervene so as to argue for the clearest course through the terrain, the general concepts of which he already took as established (modes of production, forces and relations of production, social class, etc.) but in need of clarity. Rejections of Althusser from within the Marxist tradition are often rejections on the part of political economists who do not realize that the solution to their regional debates is not the empirical correctness of their theory (since most sides in these debates, through an often crude empiricism, can produce equally convincing data), but a philosophical intervention that can tell us what position makes more sense. To be accurate: *the solution in thought* since theoretical solutions are developed, at least in the terrain of Marxism, through revolutionary struggle.

Hence, it is not Marxist political economy, Marxist historiography, or even Marxist economics that will solve those problematics that at first appear to be the region commanded by the authority of these disciplines. These disciplines are significant insofar as they provide the empirical data, mobilized according to the terrain's general logic, that contributes to the development of theory, even in a limited sense. Beyond this, they are incapable of forcing meaning—they cannot provide thorough arguments as to why one position should be accepted over another—without an appeal to something extra-economic, extra-historical, extra-theoretical. They require the reflection of philosophy, born from theory, that looks back upon the terrain that called it into being so as to argue for meaning, clarity, and force a decision in thought. When political economists argue for a specific position over another, and give reasons beyond empirical appeals, they are acting as philosophers even if they are not aware that this is the case. Althusser's significance lies in the fact that he was aware of what he was doing and thus, because of this awareness, capable of being precise.

Moreover, this slippage between theory and philosophy was already critiqued by Althusser when he spoke of how developments in the field of science produce moments of spontaneous philosophy on the part of scientists. We can add to this insight: moments of debate in political economy (take, for example, the transition debate) also result in the spontaneous practice of philosophy where political economists and historians, discovering their opponents can make the same appeals to economics and history, suddenly become quasi-philosophers; we find them attempting to justify their positions according to the extra-economic and extra-historical, some general comment on the *meaning* of the theory they are attempting to develop.[10] People are often slipping into philosophy, though not consciously, because the necessity to interpret, to demand meaning, is unavoidable. Althusser correctly understood this slippage as one that produced errors, where many scientists would tumble into the rabbit-hole of mystification in order to make sense of scientific transformations that threatened their understanding of the world.

Of course, the necessary movement to the realm of philosophy, either unconsciously or consciously, is not without its own problems. The first and most obvious problem is that we will encounter various philosophical interventions that produce competing accounts of clarity. The second problem, which might not be as obvious but follows from the first, concerns the extra-philosophical: the solution in thought might be philosophical, but it is only a solution in thought and, as such, cannot produce a real solution—that is, the transformation of reality. The solution in the "last instance" (a phrase, taken from Marx and Engels, that Althusser was fond of using) is located in revolutionary practice. Here also philosophy possesses a role—the role, though limited, of forcing us to think towards such practice—but I will discuss this in the last chapter.

But with practice and transformation in mind, I believe it is important to note that the slip into philosophy from theory, often spontaneous, is mirrored by a slippage in the opposite direction: philosophers too, when unmoored from a concrete philosophical practice, tend to become spontaneous theorists. Hence we have Deleuze and Guattari tumbling into rabbit-holes of spurious theorizing where they move uncritically from philosophical investigation to the establishment of their own subjective truth procedures, abandoning the practice of drawing lines of demarcation for the production of new concepts so as to cling to eclectic theories that are meant to establish, just for the sake of it, new provinces of theory. None of this is to say that the work of Deleuze and Guattari should be dismissed, or is wholly without merit, only that we need to be careful of the potential mystification that is caused by such a reversal.

Thus, philosophical intervention produces its own errors in its relationship with theory. Althusser's *On the Reproduction of Capitalism* is a salient example of how such errors can be made. Despite the fact that it begins with the recognition that it is an intervention located in the practice of philosophy, this book eventually attempts to force a more sophisticated articulation of the Parti Communiste Française's (PCF) revisionism in light of May 1968: Althusser eventually embraces economism (despite attacking it in earlier chapters) and electoral struggle, dismissing many of his former students as ultra-leftists. Such an error, however, should be recognized as unavoidable due to the problematic discussed in the previous chapter: in the very practice of intervening in order to force clarity, philosophers come to a given terrain with their own commitments, some of which have never been interrogated with the same philosophical precision they plan to use on another problematic. Here is where ideology intervenes spontaneously, reified as common sense, and distorts the practice of forcing clarity.

Hence, Althusser's fidelity to the ideology of the PCF would condition his philosophical intervention, undermining aspects of the clarity he sought to force. This problem, however, is largely unavoidable and was in fact anticipated by Althusser's own work on "ideological state apparatuses" and the subject. We cannot easily escape our commitments; no philosophical intervention is pure.

Clarity as demystification

Although it is perhaps impossible to avoid an absolute slippage between philosophy and theory, at the very least we can maintain some level of clarity by grasping the necessity of a distinction between the two terms—a distinction elaborated on in the first two chapters, particularly with my appeal to the concept of theoretical terrain. Clarity, especially a clarity that is demystifying, is precisely the concern of philosophy.

So we return directly to the problematic of clarity that began this chapter: philosophy remains in its proper place if the choice it attempts to clarify through its intervention is consistent with a given terrain's logic—unless it is attempting to attack a terrain's very existence, in which case the intervention is not about *clarity* but more of an antagonistic critique. Such an intervention may also perform the role of demystification for sometimes, in order to demystify a terrain, some provinces require demolition. Later we will examine the latter instance of philosophical intervention (what I will call *annihilation*), but for the moment we will persist in examining the former as well as its importance since it is the most common manner of philosophical intervention.

The reason I tend to favour the term *clarity* over the term *demystification* is because I treat the latter as a particular function of the former. Although this particular function is of utmost importance when it comes to the philosophy of Marxism, it is still a function insofar as forcing clarity may not always be about demystification. Inversely, however, demystification is always an act of clarification. For example, when we force a clear distinction between different sub-terrains of Marxism (i.e. between Trotskyism and Maoism) we are not necessarily eliminating speculative and idealist vagaries that hamper clear thinking; but when we force a distinction between an idealist and materialist manner of explaining natural causes (i.e. between explaining natural disasters as an example of God's wrath or the result of material causes), to use a very crude example, then we are bringing about clarity through demystification.

Much of enlightenment philosophy pursued clarity through this function of demystification. And yet, as Adorno and Horkheimer amongst others have noted, this practice of clarity through demystification required further demystification as it was hampered by unquestioned ideological commitments: nature was demystified but the social was not. Hence the Marxist project, a "modernity critical of modernity".[11] Philosophy as a whole still remains hampered by this mystification and, though still claiming to engage in the practice of clarity, often returns to the confused realm of speculation.

Take, for example, François Laruelle's project of *non-philosophy* that claims to be "one of the solutions that our age must contribute to the problem concerning new writings and new practices of philosophy following the age that came before it".[12] In some ways, Laruelle's project is laudable in its express attempt to produce "[r]ather than a new philosophy...a new practice of philosophy that detaches it from its own authority and includes within a thought whose origin is wholly other than philosophical...and which is also scientific rather than ontological".[13] And yet this project, regardless of whatever merits it may possess as we shall see in the following chapter, is a reinscription rather than rejection of ontological speculation.

At the very least we can agree with Laruelle when he critiques Heidegger, Deleuze, Nietzsche, and Derrida to argue, against these speculative philosophies, for a "perpetual peace treaty between science and philosophy, a treaty henceforth founded on the former rather than manipulated by the latter on its behalf, as has generally been the case in history".[14] The problem, however, is that he returns to the realm of speculative ontology, rejecting the very peace treaty he hoped to establish! Thus, despite bandying about the word "science" in multiple works, Laruelle performs the very act of non-scientific philosophical speculation he claims to reject: lacking a clear distinction between the scientific and the ideological, between the theoretical terrain and the philosophical intervention, he loses himself in speculation about the ontological foundations of science, disappearing into mystified thought that is about as "non-philosophical" as Heidegger's *Being and Time*, producing a work that is hampered by mystification and thus greatly removed from the radical popularity promised by its author.

Here again we find a philosophy (despite being cast as *non-philosophy*) misunderstanding its role: rather than actually being called into practice by theory (and most importantly *scientific* theory) regardless of what it might claim, it pretends to provide the meta-theoretical groundwork of its own terrain. An interesting eclectic project, perhaps, but speculative and mystified—significant only in that it partially understands the problem it attempts to solve while still perpetuating its mystification. More interesting, perhaps, is that the same project was promised, over a century earlier, by Ludwig Feuerbach. Feuerbach, despite the limitations of his time, understood precisely what was at stake for philosophy and its possible end. The "non-philosophy" he promised (and he used the same word), as we shall examine in the following chapter, tried hard to wash its hands of the speculative system. Grounding itself in the sensuousness of species-being, Feuerbach's project rejected the abstractions and obfuscations of philosophy to date in the name of "[*t*]*ruthfulness, simplicity, and determinateness*".[15] Laruelle's return to the problematic first conceived by Feuerbach not only comes too late—it was already shattered by the advent of the historical materialist terrain—but is guilty of the very philosophical abstractions Feuerbach saw as the problem of philosophy-qua-philosophy.

To all of these speculative philosophical projects that still exist, even if they pretend to be something other than speculative, Marxism provided an answer ages ago by seeking to put philosophy in its place and, in doing so, forcing us to think through the distinction between philosophy and theory, particularly the role of the former in relation to the latter.

Notes

1. Although I use Wittgenstein's statement in order to shed light on what I mean by philosophical practice, I want to be clear that his approach to philosophy ultimately runs counter to my own. Here I agree with Ray Brassier that Wittgenstein, like many other philosophers, maintained the primacy of philosophy over theory by assuming "that the sorts of entities and processes postulated by scientific theory are in some way founded upon, or derivative of, our more 'originally', pre-scientific understanding, whether this be construed in terms of our 'being-in-the-world' [Heidegger], or our practical engagement in 'language-games' [Wittgenstein]". (Brassier, 7) My contention is that philosophy is not foundational, that if we take it to be the logical clarification of thoughts it is a secondary practice to truth procedures operationalized by theoretical terrains. If I use Wittgenstein's definition of philosophy, and his infamous aphorism at the end of the *Tractatus*, to help explain it I do so in defiance of his anti-materialism.

2. Althusser, *Philosophy and the Spontaneous Philosophy of the Scientists*, 10.
3. Ibid.
4. Althusser, *Philosophy for Non-Philosophers*, 192.
5. Ibid.
6. Ibid., 180.
7. Hallward and Peden, *Concept and Form*, 55.
8. Rancière, *Staging the People*, 7.
9. Ibid.
10. Hence the reason why the "Political Marxists" (i.e. Robert Brenner, Ellen Meiskins Wood, etc.), in order to argue that the emergence of modern capitalism was not dependent on modern colonialism but only on the enclosure of the commons in Western Europe, make an appeal to a particular Marxist meaning of class. What is the strategy here? The realization that something more than a description of history and economic theory is required since those who reject their theoretical position are quite capable of providing the same justification. The realization that they must appeal to the *meaning of the terrain itself*, i.e. class struggle so as to argue that their position is consistent with historical materialism—that is, that their position is scientific. Since they have stumbled spontaneously into philosophy, however, they are unaware that they are even performing philosophy and are thus oblivious to what philosophy requires, the possible abandonment of their position.
11. Amin, *Eurocentrism*, 17.
12. Laruelle, *Philosophy and Non-Philosophy*, 5.
13. Ibid., 1.
14. Ibid., 21.
15. Feuerbach, 161.

Chapter Five

clarity and ontological systems

Philosophy lives on to tell the tale. Like the slave Scheherazade, it keeps forestalling death through nightly rituals of reminiscence; memory serves the project of infinite postponement. [...] Like the crumbling ruins of Carthage, the deed vanishes without a trace, the wounds heal without a scar.
Rebecca Comay, Mourning Sickness

In this chapter, with clarity in mind, I want to pause and take stock of the language and conceptual models I have so far used to think through the meaning of practising philosophy, particularly the practice of philosophy that exists because and according to the theoretical terrain initiated by Marx and Engels. Recourse to the concept of the *theoretical terrain*, and using this model in accordance to the theses I put forward in the first chapter, was simply an attempt to provide a consistent model of thought that was capable of explaining the meaning of a particular philosophical practice. When philosophy turns its gaze upon itself—makes itself the object of thought so as to explain, according to very specific political commitments, its own meaning—models are necessary so as to promote consistency. Without these models, at least in my opinion, philosophizing about philosophy will become even more confusing. That is, to avoid devolving into infinite regress (where I open myself to the possibility of making this philosophy about philosophy open to a philosophy about philosophy about philosophy, etc.), and in the interest of philosophical clarity, I have attempted to ground my investigation in an overarching conceptual language.

This conceptual language, as I indicated at the end of the second chapter, should not be taken as an ontological system.

In other words, I am not trying to argue that this model of the *theoretical terrain* is anything more than a model, an extended analogy that uses the metaphorically loose language of cartography to describe philosophy's relationship to theory, particularly the philosophy of Marxism's relationship to Marxist theory. That is, the conceptual language of the terrain is not meant to indicate a general ontology. Following Alfred Schmidt, I do not believe that Marxism possesses an ontology, in the grand and systemic sense, due to the fact that it is quite hostile to such a perspective.[1] Adorno made similar complaints in his failed attempt (mainly a failure because he was not part of any mass movement) to re-establish a Marxist philosophy: "What the conjurers of ontological philosophizing strive, as it were, to awaken is undermined by real life processes, however: by the production and reproduction of social life."[2] Real life processes infuriate ontology-qua-ontology, revealing that it is little more than a theological distortion of social relations.

But what do I mean, here, by *ontology-qua-ontology*? Ontology, simply put, is the study of being, about what it means to *be* and to *exist* in the world. This perspective is the basis of those grand philosophical systems (found in Plato, Kant, Hegel, Heidegger, etc.) that we can call ontology-qua-ontology because such a philosophical practice attempts to produce a grand interpretative gesture about the scaffolding of reality, the true world of being behind the wallpaper of appearance, and thus construct metaphysical systems. Conversely, ontological investigation in most contemporary philosophy limits itself to very precise problematics about the meaning of existence based on the presupposition that science is correct. Analytic philosophers, for example, have grappled with questions such as determination, time, and identity. Continental philosophers such as Quentin Meillassoux, whom I will discuss later in relation to this problem, have grappled with the meaning of existence following the assumption that science is correct about an "ancestral" reality of the "arche-fossil" that is "anterior to the emergence of the human species".[3] Ontology in the grand systematic sense (ontology-qua-ontology, Ontology with a capital *O*) is something quite different: an ambitious attempt to establish the foundation of reality itself, the pursuit of an extra-scientific basis for reality, that produces metaphysical categories of a speculative system which in fact distorts reality.[4]

The philosophical approach that I'm espousing—motivated by a particular gloss on Marx's eleventh thesis—forbids such a grand interpretive gesture by treating philosophy as a much more modest practice. As Morera writes:

> the approach to philosophy we should take must above all avoid the great leaps of the imagination in order to search for untenable syntheses of spirit and matter—the Hegelian ambitions to unite subject and object—and to unify in a philosophical system the disjointed experiences of peoples, for these ambitions are often the purveyors of the opium of the mind...We should set a more modest task for ourselves, one that is not only more careful but also more difficult; it is also far more useful for praxis and as a guide for building socialism.[5]

None of this is to say that Marxism lacks ontological elements, that it does not produce judgements about what it means *to be*, only that this larger and alienated question of *being*, and quandaries about the structure of reality outside of concrete instances of class struggle, are philosophical dead-ends—a way of thinking that is not materialist, that exists outside of human history, and can only hope to be an idealist abyss.

With this understanding in mind, and despite the fact that I have liberally borrowed some of his language, I do not believe that any militant philosophy with a concrete relationship to revolutionary movements and revolutionary science has much to gain from, for example, Badiou's return to ontology-qua-ontology. Although I think there are many elements in Badiou's philosophy that are useful for making philosophical interventions—concepts and language that may aid in forcing meaning and drawing distinctions—and though I cannot help but be impressed by his philosophical corpus, especially its rigour, I would still argue that he is engaged in the kind of philosophy that belongs to the realm of mystification rather than the realm of science.[6]

The construction of ontological systems is the way in which philosophy has confused itself with theory, and thus chosen to speak in the name of reality rather than understanding its proper relationship to a lived and material reality, by answering its own question—"what does it mean to exist, what does it mean to be?"—with a theory of being that is drawn from the heart of philosophical speculation. Such a practice attempts to construct the basis of reality and, in producing a new theology, deforms reality. It makes no difference whether or not our ontologist disguises their ontology under a veneer that masquerades as a respect for science: after all, if Badiou's intriguing thesis at the beginning of Being and Event is correct—that "mathematics = ontology"[7]—then he should have written no further. Instead he provided us with a massive ontological project, pushed further in Logics of Worlds, that attempts to excavate the hidden foundations of reality through philosophical speculation.

What we find in such ontological projects, then, is always an attempt to rename and reclassify the world according to purely speculative categories. Even though we should recognize the potential usefulness of the conceptual language produced by many of these projects, insofar as they may help us force clarity, we should not accept that these conceptual languages are the language of reality's deepest structures. Here is an interpretation of the world that becomes lost in its own infinitude, incapable of contributing anything by itself to transformation. The result is a conflation of philosophy with theory where, as discussed in the previous chapter, philosophy mistakes itself as a theoretical terrain. Such a conflation was inexplicable in the days before the rise of the "new sciences" where science and philosophy were often intertwined; this was why ontology-qua-ontology was paradigmatic of philosophical practice. Plato, for example, was writing in a time when natural scientists were also ontologists, when all critical approaches to reality and truth were one and the same practice. With the rise of disciplines that are capable of producing demystified truth procedures—that establish entire worlds of scientific facts and artefacts—the persistence of this old conflation is akin to a return to a supernatural explanation of natural phenomena, a deformation of a successively demystified reality.

But let us be concrete in our critique, rather than also hiding within the realm of abstract speculation, by examining a specific contemporary example of the deformation of reality produced by ontology-qua-ontology. Although I am focusing on Badiou as paradigmatic of this contemporary return to ontology, post-Marx, I have the same reservations about other ontological projects. My reason for focusing on Badiou is primarily due to the fact that Badiou is an ontologist who sees his work as part of the radical tradition initiated by Marx and Engels. Moreover, and this in some ways is to Badiou's credit, no other contemporary philosopher has succeeded in producing such a rigorous and massive ontological project since Heidegger.

Rather than assess the value of Badiou's ontology according to its own philosophical boundaries, which will in fact cause us to play the game of ontology-qua-ontology (such a criticism will in fact cause us to assess the worth of the ontological project itself rather than the worth of performing such a project), we should instead ask whether there are examples in this project where, in the interest of preserving the ontological system as a whole, reality itself is distorted and deformed. That is, the idealist nature of ontology-qua-ontology is revealed when a concrete analysis of a concrete situation becomes less important than using a concrete situation in order to demonstrate an abstract, speculative system. Hence, in *Logics of Worlds* we find a wonderful example of reality deformation that runs contrary to any limited and non-speculative intervention on the terrain of class struggle. Near the end of this book, and in order to make a series of ontological points, Badiou draws upon the concrete situation of the Oka Crisis in Québec; in doing so, he deforms the actual concrete event based on a poor assessment of the general situation.[8] What he fails to recognize is that the Kanehsatake resistance (and here he even fails to name, and thus recognize, the actual nation in revolt) was not simply unique to the "world" of Québec (he attempts to liquidate it within the especial "world" of Québec nationalism) but was more important in what it signified vis-a-vis the situation of Canadian settler-colonialism. One only needs to look back at the mainstream Canadian press to realize that the average Canadian settler, francophone and anglophone, was united in their disdain for indigenous rebellion; the very fact that the Canadian army intervened in order to contain the revolt is evidence of this fact. Moreover, if we look at the positions taken by Québecois radical organizations during the Oka Crisis we do not find, as Badiou suggests, a way in which to connect Québec nationalism with indigenous self-determination; instead we discover only a single Québecois leftist organization, Action Socialiste, siding with the Mohawk revolutionaries. And Action Socialiste, it is worth noting, would eventually produce an analysis (at the end of its existence when it reconstituted itself as the PCR-RCP) that rejected Québec nationalism as no longer relevant to the class struggle of Québec society: by 1990, this analysis claimed, aside from language differentials, Québec is no longer a unique political context different from other regional contexts in the Canadian social formation; rather, Québec was integrated with the Canadian state as a whole. The unity between

French and English settlers on the question of Oka was partial proof of this integration.

Interestingly enough, Badiou mentions the late Charles Gagnon, a former Front de Libération du Québec (FLQ) radical, in his notes on the section regarding Québec and Oka.[9] If only Badiou had traced the theoretical analysis of Québec and Canada from the Gagnon of the FLQ to the present analysis of Action Socialiste and the PCR-RCP mentioned above. Gagnon, unhappy with his former comrades' liquidation within the ranks of the Parti Québecois, would go on to form En Lutte, one of the most significant anti-revisionist Marxist-Leninist organizations of Canada's New Communist Movement. The experience of En Lutte partially influenced the experience of Action Socialiste, and both the qualities and deficiencies of Gagnon's analyses in his En Lutte period would inform the way in which Action Socialiste, and eventually the PCR-RCP, would understand indigenous self-determination in the context of a crumbling Québecois nationalism. We find a line of thought, here, that runs counter to the speculative analysis proposed by Badiou, and this line of thought explains the very "world" that Badiou cannot explain—that he is in fact deforming—in what, at times, amounts to an esoteric distortion of his object of critique. There is only one situation or world operating in the context of the Kanehsatake intifada that matters for revolutionary politics: the settler-colonial situation and, inversely, decolonization. In order to understand this we do not need to lapse into the speculative categories of *Logics of Worlds*; we only need to examine the crude material reality according to a revolutionary analysis that is itself premised on a concrete apprehension of a concrete situation.

Therefore, the Oka Crisis' meaning is not primarily located in the world of Québec, nor is its meaning located within the sphere of Québecois nationalism, as Badiou suggests through his ontological lens. These aspects do indeed provide it with a particular character, but not its universal dimension. Rather its meaning, and thus its universality, is only grasped in the fact that all of Canada (and, by correlation, both the US and Canada) is a colonial-capitalist context, and we do not require a new and rarified ontological vocabulary to explain this. When other indigenous rebellions happen in other regions and provinces the ghost of the Oka Crisis is invoked: the Six Nations rebels in Caledonia spoke of the Mohawk warriors just as the Caledonian settlers spoke of their settler Oka counterparts; the former received members of the Mohawk warriors on their barricades, the latter demanded that the Canadian state intervene in the way that it had in Québec. Even during the Oka Crisis indigenous radicals from outside of Québec were immediately involved; it is as if Badiou is ignorant of the fact that the Iroquois nation, that sees itself as a whole, is not simply located in Québec but spreads into Ontario and New York. If he had even bothered to visit Kanehsatake he would have discovered that the indigenous radicals were fluent in the languages of both their colonizers and, in fact, tended to favour English rather than French, thus putting them further beyond the pale of the "world" of Québec that he conceived.

In *Ethics* Badiou argues that the concrete particularity of a given situation explains all there needs to be known about ethical practice and that the additional "ethical" concerns that are exterior to this situation prevent this understanding. He gives an example of a doctor working within a context where there are boards devoted to "medical ethics" intended to discipline this doctor's behaviour in an "ethical" manner; his claim is that all the doctor needs to know is the "clinical situation" that demands that they treat any patient that requires help, regardless of the "ethics" of funding and proper management, if they are to actually be a doctor.[10] If we sever this examination of the "situation" from Badiou's larger ontology (despite the fact that this theory of the "situation" is meant to be a precursor to his concept of "world" used in *Logics of Worlds*) it works against his ontological project. In the situation of Oka all we need to know are the particularities of history and society, particularities that emerge from a scientific examination of the situation, and not the rarified ontological constellation Badiou forces upon the situation/world like the board of ethics in his doctor example.

Conceptual language produced by an ontological project such as Badiou's might be useful; the problem is when the structure in which it operates mystifies and obscures lived reality. If this argument is also an ontological claim, which in a very crudely semantic way it is, then it is only such insofar as it demonstrates an ontological commitment to the elimination of these much grander ontological gestures. The theoretical terrain is ontology, and the scientific terrain is ontology *par excellence*— and all this talk of "terrains" and "theory" is not an appeal to a new ontological system, but simply linguistic concepts designed for the sake of clarity. But clarity in the larger sense, not in the sense of making things so invisibly clear that they are reduced to meaningless simplicity.

If the history of analytic philosophy, despite those errors which were really no better or worse than the errors of continental philosophy, has anything to teach us, it is in its decision to banish these large-scale ontological projects to the pre-modern past. As discussed, analytic philosophers remain interested in ontology but not in ontology-qua-ontology: to ask particular questions about particular problematics of existence is not to propose another speculative system of being.

The point is to locate situations of a limited ontology (if we must use this term) and not a grand, overarching Ontology alienated from the situation. The meaning of every situation, being historical and social, can be discovered according to the science of historical materialism, that the philosophy of Marxism tails, rather than extraneous rules imposed by new speculative and ontological systems.

For while it is correct to recognize that Marxism possesses

ontological commitments, it is incorrect to assume that these commitments have much to do with ontology in the speculative sense—that systematic judgement on some deeper and hidden aspect of reality that can be found, in its purest and most recognizable form, in something like Plato's theory of forms. Physics and biology also, for instance, possess ontological commitments, and raise ontological questions, without being ontology insofar as they are not philosophy.

As we have seen, while the transformation of physics or biology might indeed produce a spontaneous philosophy, and thus a spontaneous flight back into the speculative realm where ontology-qua-ontology is constructed, it would be ludicrous to accept that the theoretical fact of, for example, the General or Special Theory of Relativity is conceptually similar to Plato's theory of forms or Heidegger's analysis of being. If we are to speak of Marxist theory as an "ontology" in the philosophical sense—and thus play the sophist—then we must say the same about every science, extending a language that developed in philosophical practice upon the non-philosophical: a category mistake that, by refusing to understand what it means, post-Marx, to interpret the world, results in the same world's deformation.

Hence, the conceptual language of the *theoretical terrain* is not an attempt to produce a systematic ontology of philosophy; it is simply a philosophical examination of philosophy, from a historical materialist position, where the concept of the terrain, and the connected language, serves as an analogical device with which to make sense of particular aspects that exist in the world and in the theoretical traditions that have been produced by people and societies in this world as a whole so as to describe concrete reality.

To speak of terrains is simply to employ a model that is useful for describing reality, and the meaning of philosophy's relationship with reality, that seeks to provide some level of consistency and coherence: to logically clarify thought. Moreover, this conceptual model is not simply about the relationship of philosophy to Marxism (though it is from this problematic that we need to begin) but about the only way in which philosophy can be practised honestly following the total demystification signified by the Marxist irruption of philosophy.

After all, the Marxist project is one that is premised on the most radical materialist understanding of reality and, because of this understanding, promises transformation: if the basic fact of the real can be grounded, not in an appeal to deep speculative structures and systems but in the motion of history and society (for all knowledge is the product of humans living in particular histories and societies and is not pre-given, is not a priori in the purest sense of the term), then to understand this motion is to understand what is necessary for historical and social transformation. The point is to understand the transformation of existence, and thus all knowledge, in a thoroughly concrete sense. There is no knowledge outside of existence, outside of actually lived societies that are embedded in history.

Again we have Althusser to thank for making this distinction clear:

> Marx opened up the 'continent of history' to scientific knowledge. He laid the groundwork for a theory constituting the foundation of all the sciences that bear on objects belonging to the 'continent of history' [...] Marx, with his discovery, provided us with scientific concepts capable, for the first time, of making intelligible what 'human societies' and their histories are—that is, of making the structure, persistence, development, stagnation and decline of societies intelligible, along with the transformations whose sites they are.[11]

A philosophical practice influenced by the Marxist terrain is the most radical practice of philosophy, despite those post-

Marxist claims to the contrary that would force us back into the realm of mystification where clarity is always compromised. Such a philosophical practice is forced, by the most thorough rejection of idealism and mystification, to tie itself to the real and act according to the function of interpretation—but an interpretation that is aware of its commitments. Already we have the "non-philosophy" that Laruelle promises after the fact, in an ambitious but misguided attempt to repeat this terrain in a manner that remains hampered by mystification. "There is in fact," Balibar argues in order to explain what he also calls a *non-philosophy*:

> no such thing [according to Marx] as an "eternal philosophy", always identical to itself: in philosophy, there are turning-points, thresholds beyond which there is no turning back. What happened with Marx was precisely a displacement of the site and the questions and objectives of philosophy, which one may accept or reject, but which is so compelling that it cannot be ignored.[12]

Unhampered by ontological speculation, interpreting the world according to class struggle, the philosophy emerging from a commitment to the Marxist terrain possesses the potential to provide the most thorough and radical clarification of reality. Here is a philosophy that can *go beyond* philosophy,[13] a philosophy that demands the clearing of the mystic ruins from every terrain, including the terrain from which it emerged.

On Feuerbach's shadow

To practise philosophy in the shadow of the eleventh thesis necessarily implies the impossibility of returning to the ontological systematization of philosophy and thus the descent into idealism. Here it is worth noting that Marx was attempting to dispel another shadow when he wrote these theses, the shadow of Ludwig Feuerbach. For it was Feuerbach, despite his inability to fully break from idealism, who also provided us with the first salient critique of such philosophy.

For Feuerbach, "speculative philosophy" (the most complete and thorough version of which, in his time, was Hegel's ontology) is ultimately "speculative theology".[14] Due to its propensity to speak about categories such as being-qua-being without grasping that such categories were premised on the fact that someone, a human philosopher embedded in the material world, was thinking them out (thus demonstrating that what is treated as *an aspect* of the speculative system is actually, in a very "sensuous" sense, *prior*) meant that these systems functioned as theological. Here, the term *theology* is not out of step with a particular philosophical tradition inherited from the ancients. Aristotle, for example, classified "first philosophy" —the study of primary principles and the causes of things—as *theologike* that, though slightly different from the term *theologia* (from which today's discipline of theology is derived), identified ontology as a study of the "divine". Feuerbach was most probably familiar with this history when he classified ontology-qua-ontology as speculative theology: he was identifying an inherent philosophical decision that was in the way of a truly humanized philosophy. That is, the categories produced by such a "theological" approach were alienated systematizations of human being, internally consistent mystified grand structures, of real people living in nature. Their supposed excavation of the grounds upon which sensuous human life existed was thus dependent on the fact that they were being built by thinking people embedded in nature who are actually incapable of going beyond the horizon of human being.[15] By masquerading as absolute—by claiming to unearth the complete meaning of being, regardless of arguments about historical unfolding—this kind of philosophy was in fact ahistorical. "Every philosophy originates, therefore," Feuerbach writes, "as a manifestation of its time; its origin *presupposes its historical time.*"[16]

In *Ludwig Feuerbach and the End of Classical German Philosophy,*
Engels notes the debt both he and Marx owed to Feuerbach's
critique of Hegel, arguing that Feuerbach's critique of
ontological systematization should lead us to recognize "an end
to all philosophy in the hitherto accepted sense of the word".[17]
At the same time, however, Engels indicates that Feuerbach did
not go far enough. In raising a prior human species being to the
level of religious sentiment, Feuerbach is wholly incapable of
understanding the materialist relations that lurk beneath his
abstract understanding of human being: "The cult of abstract
man, which formed the kernel of Feuerbach's new religion, had
to be replaced by the science of real men and of their historical
development."[18]

What is significant for our purposes, though, is that
Feuerbach represents a clearing away of philosophy as "rational
mysticism"[19]—that is a philosophy that is conflated with
theory, that exists prior to science and imagines itself as the
foundation of science itself—but in a sense that is still locked
within philosophy. Since Feuerbach was trying to defend a
materialist approach to understanding humanity and society in
a time when this science had not yet emerged, he could only
clear some of the ground necessary for such an emergence. He
was tailing something that did not yet exist and thus lacked the
ability to appreciate the event that he himself helped initiate.
As Engels points out, Feuerbach was correct in grasping the
significance of simple materialism as well as its limits; at the
same time, however, he "remained confined by the traditional
idealist fetters".[20] Thus, "[i]t was therefore a question of bringing
the science of society...into harmony with the materialist base,
and of reconstructing it on this base. But this was not granted to
Feuerbach."[21]

Now that this science exists, a terrain that should transform
the practice of philosophy itself, how can we accept a return

to the "rational mysticism" that Feuerbach, without having been "granted" the theory of historical materialism, already revealed to be backwards and contradictory? If even this quasi-materialist philosopher understood that these grand ontological projects were the perfect expression of idealism and thus ultimately opposed to any materialism and science, then how can we reconcile the persistence of this type of philosophy with the emergence and development of the terrain of historical materialism? There can be no such reconciliation except in name.

As noted at the end of the previous chapter, François Laruelle appears to be invested in Feuerbach's problematic without, for all that, having learned much from this philosopher who, like Hegel's owl of minerva, appeared at the end of German Idealism. Whereas Feuerbach brought clarity to this period of ontological speculation, demonstrating how every grand philosophical system was in fact an alienated expression of a thinking being embedded in the material world, Laruelle's project abandons clarity. Whereas Feuerbach could reject this entire approach of philosophy by demonstrating the limits of what was its consummation in Feuerbach's time—the Hegelian system—Laruelle is forced with the task of describing such a consummation in his time when philosophy, much of it already fragmented and no longer pursuing grand speculative systems, lacks this very consummation. Like Feuerbach, Laruelle begins "with non-philosophy in order through philosophy to return to non-philosophy".[22] Thus, in playing the role of a modern Feuerbach, Laruelle is forced to systematize all of philosophy up until his time into a meta-ontological system that, in his mind, is guilty of the following problem: "perpetuat[ing] the old Greek claim, that *of the sufficiency or validity of philosophy for the real, the unitary postulate of their co-belonging.* [...] The history of philosophy is that of the simultaneous or successive codings, decodings and recodings of thought and language in accordance with this postulate."[23] So a reinscription of a grand system of speculation: Laruelle builds a systematic metaphysics of demolition in his attempt to incorporate all of philosophy into a grand narrative that exists only to prefigure Laruelle.[24]

In some ways Laruelle is correct to have recognized that a certain type of philosophy may indeed code/decode/recode thought and language, locking it within a unitary system, but his insights come far too late. Not only were these insights already made by Feuerbach generations earlier—and in a far clearer and "non-philosophical" manner—but the fact that Laruelle's pronouncement happens *after* Feuerbach was eclipsed by the dawn of historical materialism means that he is writing in a context where philosophy has already been transformed, even if it often rejects this transformation. Laruelle's "non-philosophy" is nothing more than an echo of Feuerbach's project that went by the same name. Indeed, the fact is that Laruelle is simply repeating Feuerbach in his claim about a "new practice" of philosophy that treats science, rather than ontology, as its basis.[25] Feuerbach argued for the same basis: *"Philosophy must again unite itself with natural science, and natural science with philosophy.* This unity...will be more durable...than the previous *mésalliance* between philosophy and theology."[26] *Theology*, here, meaning ontology. This was his philosophy of the future, a "new philosophy" akin to Laruelle's "new practice of philosophy". The similarities are astounding, but far less astounding than the fact that Feuerbach was clearer and more direct than his modern avatar.

The advent of historical materialism, however, casts an entire shadow over this project. In criticizing philosophy and demanding a new philosophy that was the inverted non-philosophy of the previous system-building, Feuerbach was still seeking the answers of reality in philosophy itself no matter what he said about science. His project was a mystified understanding of the terrain and philosophy as a later, interpretive gesture; it assimilated philosophy with the terrain, arguing that the solution was in the construction of a new non-speculative system. Laruelle makes the same mistake but with historical hindsight: a return to Feuerbach's project that is simultaneously a step backwards in its fetishization of a formal speculative system. But we shall return to this error in the following chapter, tracing it out through Laruelle's later work, in light of the problematic of clarity and the ruins of grand ontological projects.

Occultation (1)

Ontological systematization, however, is simply part of a larger tendency in philosophy: *occultation*. That is, the tendency or philosophical practice to render thought obscure and esoteric. To be clear, it is indeed the case that intellectual labour in areas of rigorous philosophical abstraction make comprehension and engagement difficult for those without the requisite training. The fragmentation of knowledge is such that entire areas of study will be opaque to the layperson and that every philosophical or academic specialist will be a layperson in many areas outside of their expertise. Debates in rarified fields of symbolic logic may seem incomprehensible, for example, to thinkers trained in social philosophy just as the work of experts in particle physics might be inaccessible for practitioners of microbiology.

Thus, occultation is not the unavoidable problem of training and abstract specialization; as human knowledge increases the ability to know anything about entire vistas of thought becomes a fact of existence. In *Stars In My Pocket Like Grains of Sand*, Samuel Delany describes a future intergalactic civilization that faces the threat of "Cultural Fugue" due to the fact that the breadth of human knowledge has increased to such a level that even sets of facts and strings of data we once took to be common sense have become unknowable to hundreds of thousands of people. "If only there is so much to know in our human universe," Delany explains his fiction of future knowledge fragmentation, "the working assumption you can go on is: You can assume, *about absolutely any fact*...that nine hundred and ninety-nine people out of a thousand do *not* know it—which goes for the working assumption too...[I]n our human universe, of necessity, *all* facts are as little known as the works of great poets."[27]

But it is due to this undeniable process of knowledge fragmentation, the extreme variant being Delany's fictional "fugue", that occultation becomes a tempting philosophical practice. Recognizing that investigation in levels of philosophical abstraction is opaque to the layperson and that this layperson has started to believe that, because of this fragmentation, philosophy is synonymous with esoteric thought, there is the impulse to abandon all attempts at demystification and clarity. The tendency, here, is to render philosophical investigation even more opaque and obscure, producing work intended only for a specialized audience, and thus to become part of the knowledge fugue that philosophy should otherwise seek, no matter how difficult, to prevent.

Philosophy thus possesses two practical tendencies: demystification and occultation. While the former tendency possesses a long history that stretches back to Socrates if not further, and is the tendency that a Marxist practice of philosophy should embrace, the latter also possesses its primordial precedents. As far as we know many of the pre-Socratics were driven by the desire to occult thought, functioning as mystics who guarded, with their obscure pronouncements, knowledge that was to be available only to the enlightened few: the Pythagorean cult is a perfect example. We can find similar individuals and traditions throughout the ancient world over a variety of cultures whose esoteric pronouncements were called philosophy; occultation is not alien to philosophy but, in fact, the obfuscating shadow of the demystifying tendency. I have chosen to privilege the latter because of the importance I place on the Marxist rupture.

This occultation persists. Even worse, it persists in philosophy that is deemed radical. For example, in his now infamous interview with *Reason* magazine, John Searle claimed:

> With Derrida, you can hardly misread him, because he's so obscure. Every time you say, "He says so and so," he always says, "You misunderstand me." But if you try to figure out the correct interpretation, then that's not so easy. I once said this to Michel Foucault, who was more hostile to Derrida even than I am, and Foucault said that Derrida practiced the method of *obscurantisme terroriste* (terrorism of obscurantism). [...] And I said, "What the hell do you mean by that?" And he said, "He writes so obscurely you can't tell what he's saying. That's the obscurantism part. And then when you criticize him, he can always say, 'You didn't understand me; you're an idiot.' That's the terrorism part."[28]

Philosophers such as Derrida gain followings not primarily because of the content of their work which, when deciphered, is largely unremarkable. Their status as philosophical grey eminences is mainly due to the esoteric nature of their form: the more obscure something is, claims the acolyte of occultation, the more *profound* and thus more philosophical it must be. Most importantly, the more enlightened few—those specialists who become the interlocutors of its obscurantism—it can produce, the more it can retain its aura of significance.

Heidegger is perhaps the paradigm example of occultation. Brassier has pointed out that Heidegger's obscurantism is such that his philosophical accounts "unfold entirely in the domain of hermeneutic sense" so as to "outweigh" the clarifying concerns of "rigour" and "stringency".[29] The result is that Heidegger can assert a philosophical system of interpretation (a hermeneutics) axiomatically and without any prior justification, describe its boundaries, and then "castigate those who would deny it".[30] Heidegger thus produces an occult system that functions according to its own interior rules but without any logical justification for these rules: it reads as profound because of its obscure hermeneutics. It is Laruelle's philosophical decision par excellence.

These days it is becoming increasingly difficult to be a Heideggerian and deny the intrinsic connection between Heidegger's philosophical labour and Nazi ideology. But even without Heidegger's own admission that his philosophy was a defence of National Socialism the relationship should be obvious: Heidegger's fascination with an obscure/mystified hermeneutics of existence is an occult practice, not that different from the kind of boundaries drawn by an Aleister Crowley, and the Nazis too were obsessed with occultation. To produce an order of thought that requires an "obscure subject" as its locus is the business of fascism.[31]

But the Marxist practice of philosophy is determined by its political decision to align with the masses against the division of mental and manual labour. Hence, this practice represents the most radical variant of the philosophical tendency to demystify, clarify, and force meaning. Knowledge should be exoteric rather than esoteric. Occultation must be resisted and such a resistance will necessarily declare all obscurantist philosophies, no matter their radical pretensions, occult wagers that, along with the obscure subject they produce, are worthy of the dustbin of history.

Occultation (2)

In *After Finitude* Quentin Meillassoux suggests that there might be something deeply wrong with a philosophical practice that seeks to uncover the metaphysical scaffolding of reality—indeed, something deeply wrong with the normative practice of speculative philosophy from Kant onwards. This problem, which he calls "correlationism", can be explained in the following manner: there is no way to understand the world outside of our own conscious apprehension of the world since to speak meaningfully of the world is to speak of it according to the categories of our consciousness; since there is no way to know the world *as it really is outside of human existence* without getting "out of our own skins"[32] all we can do is speak of the world as it is *for us* rather than it is in itself—it is in fact "naive" or "pre-critical" to assume we can speak meaningfully of the latter. Hence, according to the correlationist perspective, it is philosophically impossible to make any meaningful statements about a world anterior to human consciousness since it could not be logically admitted as a *world*. That is, without conscious beings to be aware that "this is the world" no meaningful world can exist, or meaningful understanding of such a world can exist.

The problem, however, is that contemporary science makes claims about a world anterior to human existence. First of all, physics asserts an "ancestrality" of the anterior by making meaningful scientific statements about a pre-human existence according to non-human objective statements about time: the "origin of the universe" is dated at 13.5 billion years ago; the "accretion of the earth" is dated at 4.56 billion years ago.[33] Secondly, biology and archaeology assert the concept of "the arche-fossil" where the fossil record predating human existence also produced meaningful statements: the origin of pre-sentient life on earth is dated at 3.5 billion years ago, the origin of humanity at 2 million years ago, and "the coming into being of consciousness and its spatio-temporal forms of givenness in the midst of a space and time which are meant to pre-exist" humanity's conscious apprehension of space and time.[34] That is, scientists can speak meaningfully of an evolutionary process that not only predates consciousness but is foundational to the emergence of consciousness. Scientists do not make these statements in a qualified philosophical manner; they do not add the "codicil" that, for example, the accretion of the earth happened 4.56 billion years ago *for us*. They mean these statements quite literally and believe that they can objectively, even absolutely, describe a world without human consciousness. According to contemporary speculative philosophy, however, such a claim should not be possible since it is treated as philosophically impossible to describe a world outside of the categories of human consciousness. Hence contemporary science is philosophically naive.

Therefore, since Kant, philosophy has inherited a mechanics of logic and phenomenology that is deeply invested in occultation. Rather than accept various scientific terrains as the grounds of truth procedures, because of a conceptualization of human conscious experience that knits everything into a correlationist circle, philosophy has sought to become the scaffolding of every science. Philosophers in both the analytic and continental traditions claim to inform scientists about what they are "really saying" about reality while, perhaps hypocritically, attempting to preserve scientific truth claims:

> Thus, a philosopher will generally begin with an assurance to the effect that her theories in no way interfere with the work of the scientist, and that the manner in which the latter understands her own research is perfectly legitimate. But she will immediately add (or say to herself): legitimate, *as far as it goes*. What she means is that although it is normal, and even natural, for the scientist to adopt a spontaneously realist attitude, which she shares with the "ordinary person", the philosopher possesses a specific type of knowledge which imposes a correction upon science's ancestral statements—a correction which seems to be minimal, but which suffices to introduce us to another dimension of thought in its relation to being.[35]

The entire philosophical project of providing speculative scaffolding that is prior to scientific claims, that can provide a deeper meaning to the truth procedures of the sciences, is thus based on this correlationist conceit. The impulse to occult emerges from a philosophical arrogance. Every form of mystification springs from the desire to tell a story about reality as it truly is beyond the "naive" materialist descriptions provided by science, to fix science upon philosophical foundations. While it is indeed the case that this seems to make sense according to the logical boundaries drawn by science (i.e. how can we conceptualize the world anterior to human consciousness if we can't get out of our own conscious apprehension of the world), this sensibility is a decision inherent to a particular type of philosophical magical thinking.

The story Meillassoux tells about "ancestrality" and "the arche-fossil" vis-a-vis philosophy is another variant of our narrative of the theoretical terrain and the practice of philosophy. The ancestral and the arche-fossil represent the truth procedures of scientific terrains; a materialist approach to philosophy would do well to accept claims of these types according to their own terms and limit intervention to making sense of them according to the boundaries they draw. The impulse of the philosophical decision, though, is to instead occult by attempting to provide a deeper layer of reasoning, a scaffolding behind the terrain— to ontologically systematize what is presented to us by science according to an absurd philosophical reasoning inherited from Kant's Ptolemaic counter-revolution. Philosophy-as-such is forced to reject materialism *tout court*:

> Confronted with the arche-fossil, *every variety of idealism converges and becomes equally extraordinary*—every variety of correlationism is exposed as an extreme idealism, one that is incapable of admitting that what science tells us about these occurrences of matter independent of humanity effectively occurred as described by science. And our correlationist [or "our philosopher"] then finds herself dangerously close to

contemporary creationists.[36]

This correlationism is extensive; its influence on philosophical thinking goes beyond the problem of the anterior outlined by Meillassoux. Everything in existence, the entire material world and practical experience, is its domain, material to be captured and occulted. Take, for example, categories significant to the scientific terrain of historical materialism: property, appropriation, production, consumption. Philosophers in the Heideggerian tradition, such as Jean-Luc Nancy and Giorgio Agamben, have spent their careers attempting to demonstrate that Marxism is naive because it does not understand the deeper meaning behind these categories, that the "social philosophy" of Marxism is undermined by a secret commitment to property since the praxis it espouses is invested in collective appropriation—therefore still invested in the *proper* (because property and appropriation are linguistically related), and therefore unable to break from an ontology of property relations, the so-called problem of the *dispotif*.[37] Hence a hermeneutical circle is drawn around scientific categories so as to provide speculative justification that, like the "codicils" added to claims about ancestrality, are intended to provide a metaphysical bedrock of meaning beneath a terrain's truth procedure.

But the historical materialist categories designated as material for excavation by these philosophers are not speculative. Like the problem of ancestrality and the arche-fossil these social categories are only a problem if they are occulted. Marx and Engels were not putting forth philosophical concepts designated for philosophical excavation but concepts that were part of a scientific terrain. To claim that "the expropriation of the expropriators" is philosophically naive because there is a deeper meaning of property is the same as claiming that scientific proclamations about the anterior cannot be literal. In a revolution private property can and should be expropriated and any philosophical authority that seeks to question the meaning of "property" beyond the masses' desire to pull down the grand exploiter will find themselves lost in the dust of historical momentum. The fact that anyone would seek to occult something that is so visceral, and believe that this occultation matters in the struggle for historical momentum is the height of philosophical arrogance.

To be both a materialist and a philosopher requires the rejection of this occultation, this attempt to provide metaphysical "codicils" to scientific claims. If this renders philosophy "naive" and "pre-critical" then so be it: the world described by a philosophy that seeks to occult the theoretical terrain is a world determined by magical thinking, an invented pseudo-foundation to meaning itself. But faced with this occultation, and in an effort to reject it, other philosophical mistakes can emerge: the assimilation to or betrayal of the theoretical terrain.

Assimilation and betrayal

All things considered, and once the mystic ruins (which include the ruins of contemporary "rational mysticisms") are cleared from innumerable theoretical terrains, we can pursue a project of clarification in which the practice of philosophy is limited to making sense of a terrain's logic according to its interior logic and the political commitment from which this project emerges. The forcing of clarity, however, does not always proceed according to this interior logic. A critical, consistent and clear intervention, though attempting to clarify a choice according to a terrain's own logic, always operates (as discussed in the previous chapter) according to the class position and theoretical fidelity of the philosopher. That is, a philosophical intervention is already conditioned, and needs to be aware of this conditioning, but should also be aware of this conditioning in the context of the interior logic of what it is attempting to clarify. Here, there are two possible mistakes that may produce a lack of clarity:

i) losing oneself in the logic of the terrain under investigation so that the terrain's logic becomes the philosophical conditions; ii) ignoring the terrain's logic—that is, its historical truth procedure(s)—so that it is eclipsed and betrayed by one's prior theoretical conditioning.

The first mistake, which I call *assimilation*, is one that is often the result of an uncritical fidelity to a terrain's truth procedure. In the case of Marxism, for example, a Marxist's philosophical intervention upon the field of Marxism would obviously be conditioned by fidelity to this terrain—this is, perhaps, a rather banal point. At the same time, however, one's fidelity to Marxism as a whole can become confused with the interior logic of a region within the overall terrain; this is where the intervention becomes mistaken and, in a moment of total assimilation, fails to produce clarity. For when we intervene within Marxist sub-terrains, usually in order to clarify what is at stake in a regional debate (i.e. the question of transition, the large debates between different Marxist trajectories, the meaning of the theory of value, the conception of class war, etc.) and hopefully force a decision, we do this by asserting the larger conditions of the terrain. By doing so, however, we may end up becoming subsumed in the interior logic of these debates to the extent that we cannot draw demarcating lines according to an archimedian point. Such an assimilation is always a danger, particularly if we mistake our commitment to a position within a regional debate as our fidelity to the terrain as a whole. For example, many of those committed to a very doctrinaire understanding of communism during the 1960s—where the Communist Party of the Soviet Union was understood to possess the authority of the international Comintern—were too assimilated to a specific trajectory of this terrain's interiority to recognize that they were actually acting against the way in which the Marxist terrain should be understood, that they were "revisionists". Utterly assimilated within the terrain they could no longer ask the larger questions regarding meaning and clarity.

All critical interventions within the Marxist terrain (that is, those that have produced clarity and aided theoretical development) have been interventions that, though proclaiming fidelity to the terrain's overall logic, have refused to assimilate themselves so as to become dogmatic and formulaic. If we do not retain some position from which to judge a given terrain's development how can we properly assess whether it is developing according to its logic, how can we even name this logic? While it is correct to note that we will be, and always are, theoretically assimilated (we are never, as aforementioned, unconditioned) to some extent, we must also retain some level of exterior conditioning from which to examine these interior logics. Take, for example, the terrain of biology in the nineteenth century and the development of racial sciences: those philosophers who lost themselves in the conditions of the biological terrain at that point and time simply ended up being assimilated according to a truth procedure that was still in question and, in this assimilation, adapted their thought according to theoretical language that, by itself, would lead to an acceptance of precisely what needed to be called into question: physiognomy, phrenology, etc. Here, lines of demarcation would be drawn according to the very logic that needed to be demarcated.

The second mistake, which I will label *betrayal*, is common for Marxists to make. For there are times when we want a theoretical terrain's essential logic to look precisely like the logic of the terrain that has conditioned our thought and thus intervene with this desire in mind without necessarily realizing that such an intervention will undermine the terrain's truth procedure. The orthodox Marxist claim that "dialectics" is something that can be found in the natural world is a claim that often lends itself to this betrayal: when a science's historical procedure of truth does not appear to be properly "dialectical" then, based on our commitment to this formula, we can simply dismiss a particular trajectory of truth, regardless of its interior importance, because it does not accord to our exterior conditioning. We want this terrain to look precisely like our terrain and, when it does not, we attempt to intervene and draw demarcating lines that betray the truth processes we wish to investigate.

Hence, those Marxists who have dismissed key developments in the terrain of physics—such as the Big Bang theory, dark matter, and everything else that was initially unlocked by the Einsteinian moment of rupture-continuity—because they *appear* to be in contradiction with the Marxist terrain (but are in fact only in contradiction with particular mappings of this terrain) are betraying the terrain they claim to be supporting. While it is important to note that such interventions can and should be conditioned by the logic of historical materialism, such a conditioning should not mean the eclipse of another terrain's logic. We rightfully mock those religious philosophers who apply the logic of theology to science so as to dismiss evolution; we correctly prefer those theologians whose intervention on the same terrain, though qualified by their fidelity to x religion, is performed in a manner that does not undermine the truth value of evolution but, rather, seeks to interpret this truth according to their terrain's own processes.[38] Thus, we should also critique those Marxist philosophers who wield the theology of an abstract "dialectical materialism" against other scientific terrains.[39]

To betray a terrain is to ignore its logic by forcing it to accord to what we want its logic to be; it is to deny its development, and even act against this development, like a cartographer who is attempting to draw a route imported from another country upon a territory they have never surveyed simply because they are comfortable with this route.[40] When Marxists argue, for example, that we should ignore the great revolutionary movements because of some Platonic notion of *real* communism ("Communism should look like x and because real-world communist movements did not look like x they are not *true communism"*) they are actually betraying the terrain by assessing its interior logic according to an ideology that is opposed to this very terrain. They betray their commitments in the very act of speaking for them, collaborating with the deformation of history in the process. Alternately, a mirror act of betrayal is enacted when Marxists defend "actual existing socialisms" that have veered into revisionist territory: while it may look like they are chastising those who betray the terrain in the interest of purity— as discussed above—they are in fact defending social formations on the capitalist road by refusing to accept what the terrain tells us about revolution: it will be messy and impure, yes, but it will always be in danger of falling to capitalist restoration. There may be a fine line separating moralistic betrayal and scientific criticism, but the demarcation is earth-shatteringly significant.

Of course we do not have to deal solely with the Marxist terrain to understand assimilation and betrayal. The same mistakes leading to a lack of clarity can happen within other theoretical terrains. An assimilation within the particular theological terrain of Christianity, for example, is evinced in Luther's rejection of Muntzer's radicalism based on Luther's assumption that his understanding of the terrain, though conditioned by his class position, defined the terrain itself; a betrayal is the emergence of Mormonism, based on the importation of an anti-Christian logic that attempted to remake this terrain according to a new (but terribly impoverished) image. An assimilation within a particular aesthetic terrain is the dictum of "art for art's sake"—an assimilation into the sphere of art that does nothing for art but reduce it to the most regionalist understanding of its unfolding geography—whereas a betrayal would be the crudest form of activist art, the ugliest and most predictable example of didacticism. Most importantly: an assimilation within a particular "hard" scientific terrain is a refusal to accept development beyond particular theoretical standards (i.e. the past Newtonian who rejects the Einsteinian/post-Einsteinian present); a betrayal is the importation of mysticism so as to make sense of a paradigm shift.

Forcing clarity

As discussed throughout this chapter, the vast majority of philosophical interventions are concerned with the problematic of clarity. Such interventions are intended to force meaning by clarifying the grounds of a debate within a given terrain. Although this practice might not seem entirely grand, it has historically led to what the post-structuralists have deemed "grand narratives"; the very ontologies we have critiqued have also been built upon these interventions. Plato's intervention in the field of ancient mathematics, for example, led directly to the *Republic*. Kant and Hegel's intervention in the early modern sciences led to their own respective ontologies. Are these also moments where the philosopher endorses the temptation to slip into the role of the theorist? Perhaps, but this slippage may also be unavoidable; successive philosophical interventions are required to clarify the meaning of such transgressions.

The importance of clarity, however, should not be underestimated; it may be the result of following, and being conditioned by, various theoretical terrains but it is also a practice that brings these terrains to life. We only need to examine the terrain of aesthetic/art theory in order to appreciate the clarifying role of philosophy. Benjamin's *The Work of Art in the Age of Mechanical Reproduction*, Rancière's *The Future of the Image*, and especially Mao's *Talks at the Yenan Forum on Art and Literature* are instances of philosophical intervention intended to clarify the terrain. (To these we can add Aristotle's *Poetics*, though severely conditioned by the artistic practices of the ancient world.) These philosophical interventions are all useful in clarifying the meaning of art and what it means to engage in artistic practice. When we look at a piece such as *Rent Collection Courtyard* (1965), for example, and ask what this precursor to the modern installation meant in a revolutionary context approaching the Cultural Revolution, we are producing questions that demand philosophical clarification.[41]

A theoretical terrain and the theorists engaged in a given terrain are not philosophers, though they may at times pretend to engage in this practice (or even spontaneously do so), and thus may require a philosophical intervention. Therefore, as aforementioned, some debates can and will require philosophical intervention if they are to ever move beyond a theoretical impasse where both sides appeal to the same terrain, submerge themselves in a crude empiricism that produces equally powerful justification, and lack the ability to think outside of their boxes. Here I am thinking of debates over the labour theory of value, the question of transition, the theory of a labour aristocracy, and other contested theoretical regions: I believe that the labour theory of value is correct, that the "Political Marxists" are wrong about the theory of transition, and that there is such a thing as the labour aristocracy precisely because these are questions that can only be answered by a philosophical intervention. Those who I take to be on the wrong side of these debates are also those who end up making philosophical pronouncements without being aware of what it means to practise philosophy: they are guilty of assimilation or betrayal.

No clarity is produced in those political and economic terrains that are locked in a seemingly endless struggle over the question of these terrains' truth procedures; the philosopher can and should help clarify the grounds of these debates and force a choice, sometimes even clearing away the mystic cobwebs that hamper thought. Such a clarification, if it pursues demystification while avoiding assimilation and betrayal, will hopefully force a choice according to the terrain's interior logic. Some of these militant theorists, oft-times dedicated to a position that revolts against this forcing, will despise the judgement—but this is to be expected. After all, those biologists dedicated to the sciences of phrenology and physiognomy also despised philosophical judgement; now they belong to the mausoleums of history.

Notes

1. In *The Concept of Nature in Marx*, Schmidt claims that Marxist materialism possesses a "non-ontological character". (19)
2. Adorno, *Negative Dialectics*, 65.
3. Meillassoux, 10.
4. I do not mean, either here or elsewhere, "speculative" in the sense utilized by Meillassoux to distance himself from idealist and correlationist "metaphysics" but in the sense utilized by Feuerbach when he called Hegel's ontology "speculative theology".
5. Morera, *Gramsci, Materialism, and Philosophy*, 27.
6. This tendency of a certain type of philosophy to obfuscate reality by recourse to speculative categories that actually fail to clarify thought in a meaningful sense is one of the reasons why analytic philosophers (who, to be fair, are usually interested in much more boring concerns) generally, and maybe unfairly, treat contemporary continental philosophy as pseudo-philosophy.
7. Badiou, *Being and Event*, 6.
8. Badiou, *Logics of Worlds*, 303-324.
9. Ibid., 542.
10. Badiou, *Ethics*, 14-15.
11. Althusser, *On the Reproduction of Capitalism*, 18.
12. Balibar, *The Philosophy of Marx*, 5.
13. Ibid., 4.
14. Feuerbach, 151.
15. Ibid. 53-96.
16. Ibid., 59.
17. Engels, *Ludwig Feuerbach und the End of Classical German Philosophy*, 11.
18. Ibid., 38.

19. Feuerbach, 86.
20. Engels, *Ludwig Feuerbach and the End of Classical German Philosophy*, 25.
21. Ibid.
22. Schmidt, 24.
23. Laruelle, *Philosophy and Non-philosophy*, 3.
24. I am aware that, so far, I am referring mainly to Laruelle's early work and that, since *Philosophy and Non-philosophy*, his "non-philosophical" project has gone through a variety of rearticulations. It is my contention, however, that all of these rearticulations are still based on the assumption that philosophy up until Laruelle is a singular prior decision that either takes the form of transcendence or immanence. I will examine these rearticulations in a later chapter; for now it is appropriate to think about the meaning of non-philosophy and how it relates to Feuerbach's earlier project.
25. Ibid., 1.
26. Feuerbach, 172.
27. Delany, 141.
28. http://reason.com/archives/2000/02/01/reality-principles-an-intervie
29. Brassier, 161.
30. Ibid., 162.
31. Badiou, *Logics of Worlds*, 61.
32. Meillassoux, 11.
33. Ibid., 9.
34. Ibid., 21.
35. Ibid., 13.
36. Ibid., 18.
37. For a thorough analysis of these philosophers' work on this problematic, along with Roberto Esposito's contributions, Greg Bird's *Containing Community* (New York: State University of New York Press, 2016) is highly recommended. Although Bird seems, at times, to be similarly invested in

this philosophical decision of occultation, and often puts too much significance in the hermeneutical games of these thinkers, his work is the most precise and rigorous critical exposition of this particular post-Heideggerian trend. Moreover, to be fair to Bird and despite my disagreements with what he takes to be significant, *Containing Community* is guided by a sensibility that is far more activist and openly anti-capitalist than the work he's discussing. Indeed, Bird's concern that property relations run deeper than the anti-capitalist left tends to believe, and that this problem might undermine resistance movements, makes his thoughts on these thinkers more significant than the thinkers themselves.

38. See, for example, the work of the theologian Peter Enns who, though a Christian who accepts the "Apostles' Creed" and the general Christian narrative, also completely accepts the Darwinian theory of evolution as well as a lot of historical science around textual criticism, archaeology, and ethics.

39. A good example of this problem is *Reason in Revolt* by Alan Woods and Ted Grant that I have criticized, for this very reason, in *Continuity and Rupture*.

40. An interesting side note: the Situationists believed the practice of literally displacing geographical routes was politically progressive (i.e. using a map of Paris to explore London) because it would allow us to appreciate the ways in which space is structured by capitalism. Aside from being an interesting art project, which has its own regional truth procedures, I'm of the opinion this practice is little more than avant garde tourism. As a political practice psychogeography is useless: we need to accurately map the city in which we reside in order to embark on social investigation, mass work, and organization; we need to understand the actual geography for demonstrations and militant interventions—following the map of Paris in the midst of a demonstration in the streets of London will most probably result in mass

arrests.

41. The artistic sequence initiated by *Rent Collection Courtyard* remains contemporary and can be traced to the work of artists such as Michael Elmgreen and Ingar Dragset, most notably their *Welfare Show* (2005) installation.

Chapter Six

philosophy and annihilation

The crisis consists precisely in the fact that the old is dying and the new cannot be born; in this interregnum a great variety of morbid symptoms appear.
Antonio Gramsci, Prison Notebooks

Although the practice of philosophy is primarily concerned with clarifying theoretical impasses, it is sometimes also concerned with demolishing and delegitimizing particular theories. (Sriduangkaew's analogy that began this book is thus apt: the denouement machine in her story, which I suggested represented the operation of philosophy, laid siege to the terrain in which it operated by targeting the former's own logic.) Although such a demolition is often intended to promote some level of clarity, there are also moments where the demolition is so thorough that it functions primarily according to a logic of annihilation rather than clarity. Philosophy should be understood as a practice that, in the last instance, is performed in the service of the terrain— as I argued at the conclusion of the second chapter—it may often be the case that philosophy is serving the larger terrain by demanding the eradication of an interior province, or even serving another terrain by demanding the demolition of a terrain that the philosopher believes should not exist even theoretically (i.e. the philosopher of astronomy demanding the annihilation of astrology).

The best-known variant of this annihilationist philosophy is Nietzsche's project with its sustained and undisguised attempt to "philosophize with a hammer" by attacking numerous theoretical terrains from which the philosophy of Nietzsche's time had emerged. Here we have to be careful not to confuse what I mean by *annihilation* with *nihilism*, though they share the same etymology. Nietzsche was clearly not a nihilist: while he saw its emergence as an inevitable result of the "death of God", he also treated it as a symptomatic problem rooted in the same order he desired to demolish. Nietzsche's focus, whatever its problems, was on discovering the foundations upon which certain theoretical terrains rested and, since he found these terrains immeasurably sick, intervening philosophically so as to demand the demolition of these foundations altogether. In this sense he was not precisely an *anti-philosopher*—which is to say, following Badiou's categorization, a *sophist*—but the kind of philosopher entirely focused on the elimination of very specific theoretical terrains. Perhaps this concern caused Nietzsche to lapse into those practices that can rightly be called anti-philosophy (i.e. rhetorical ploys, the raising of the aesthetic over the political, the homogenization of history) but I believe it is more accurate to think of him as a philosopher who was obsessed with the practice of demolition and annihilation.

Hence, the Nietzschean project's significance is not in its supposed descent into this so-called anti-philosophy but in what it can tell us about the limits of that philosophy which is focused primarily on annihilation. That is to say: a philosophical practice primarily based on the annihilation of theoretical terrains is one that, by assuming it has the power to demolish and rebuild a given terrain, is most often ignorant of the position from which it wages this war of annihilation. We can say, here, that the pure practice of philosophical annihilation is one that, by assuming (either explicitly or implicitly) that it possesses the power to call any and every theoretical terrain into question—thus striking at the roots of whatever it finds repellant—is already assimilated into those terrains that, by virtue of an ignorance and/or unconscious fidelity, it fails to apprehend. Therefore, such an annihilationist practice functions according to the axiom, established in the third chapter, of political commitment; the problem, however, is that such a practice, when it is assumed to be pure, is unable to recognize the meaning of this commitment.

This inability to grasp the basis of one's own commitment often results in a misapprehension of the theoretical terrain that is intended for demolition due to an inability to realize the reasons behind the act of demolition. Nietzsche thus attacked the basis of what had become, in his day, enlightenment thought without understanding that he was committed to the most repellant problems of the enlightenment—the purist form of bourgeois ideology, an unconscious commitment to this class's imaginary. In *Dialectic of Enlightenment*, for example, Horkheimer and Adorno interpret Nietzsche's project as an auto-critique of the European Enlightenment insofar as it was criticizing the supposed basis of this discourse from the position of its most extreme logic.[1] All of Nietzsche's complaints about slave-morality and the rot that supposedly hindered Western civilization, then, were eerily similar (though arguably exaggerated) to the complaints that a conscious bourgeois subject would make of the problems that stood in the way of unhindered capitalism: collectivity, the rejection of the pure and isolated individual, "slavish" solidarity. Here the demolition becomes a tired valorization of precisely those values that were emerging as common sense—an unconscious reification of that theoretical terrain that actually *does* require demolition.

To Nietzsche we can add, with some honourable exceptions, the entire post-modern and post-structuralist turn in philosophy that is marked by the same tendency of annihilationism. In their obsession to do away with those "grand" and "totalizing" narratives—those discourses of power-knowledge that dare to speak in the name of science and are thus murderous in their speaking—such philosophies were acting according to a grander and far more totalizing narrative that could easily endure such questioning because it had achieved hegemony. For capitalism, just before the ascendance of post-modern philosophy, had declared itself the end of history; all assaults on those grand narratives that questioned its ascendancy were encouraged and, in this encouragement, any critique of its own totalization could be endured.

Any hegemony will consent to some form of critique, as long as this critique is also levelled at those ideologies that concretely threaten its existence, because it has little to fear from a practice limited to the realm of philosophy. When it is claimed that all organized and militant challenges that take the form of a revolutionary party (a universal political order raised against the failed universalism of capitalism), as well as theories of revolutionary strategy and mass mobilization, are as murderous and totalizing as the current state of affairs, then there arises (as with every philosophical intervention) a declaration of meaning that parallels the very meaning of the hegemonic regime. If, as the post-modern and neo-Nietzschean variant of annihilationist philosophy declares, all revolutionary challenges to capitalism are themselves suspect, then what meaning is there in a theoretically and practically organized rebellion that consciously and systematically seeks to perform an act of *concrete* rather than *speculative* annihilation? Here the totalizing critique of a supposedly pure annihilationist philosophy fails to deliver on its promise: in its extreme focus on annihilation it ends up reifying the ruling ideas of the ruling class.

The impossibility of pure annihilation

A purely annihilationist philosophy is impossible; those who think they are embarking on such a project end up reaffirming precisely what should be annihilated—the "common sense" ideology of the ascendant hegemony that is always, at the very moment they think they are outside of its command, imported into their practice. But once we move beyond such philosophical purity (and we must, as previously discussed, be suspicious of those philosophies that act as if they are unconditioned) we can conceptualize an annihilationist practice that does not proceed from a position of bad faith. For philosophy can and should play, in specific historical moments, this annihilatory role: while it is impossible to do so in the Nietzschean manner without performing a parallel act of ideological reification, we should endorse the practice of "philosophizing with a hammer" when it is demanded by a particular historical conjuncture.

I do not think it is an entirely controversial point to assert that there are theoretical terrains and provinces that deserve annihilation rather than clarification. While it may be correct to premise annihilation on the basis of clarification (that is, recognize that the decision of annihilation is possible only after the practice of clarification/demystification since we will learn what needs to be annihilated by clarifying the terms in question), it is not incorrect to recognize that there are times in which clarification will lead us to the necessity of demolition... And oft-times demolition will be an act of grand demystification. Once again we can speak of those flawed biological provinces of racial science that, after being forced into clarity and found wanting, necessitated an intervention that was annihilationist. While it is correct to assert that philosophy is *an interpretive gesture that investigates and reflects on problems encountered in a theoretical terrain* (as noted in the first chapter's fifth proposition), interpretation can be aimed at gesturing violently against the very basis of a terrain, province, or region. That is, aimed at demanding annihilation. If such a demand is met in concrete practice reality as a whole will be further demystified—freed from a presence that is perniciously idealist.

Philosophy in its annihilationist guise is thus the philosophy of the negative critique, the polemic, the interpretive gesture designed to force a decision between two theoretical terrains: one that will be devalorized in the interests of possible demolition, another that will be valorized as the salient option. All the tools of philosophy designed to promote clarity and demystification—the argument, logic, auto-critique, etc.—will be brought to bear upon a terrain or convention, marking it with a condemned sign. This is not a particularly radical practice: for example, J.S. Mill's *The Subjection of Women* is a liberal example of annihilationist philosophy (it brings the tools of philosophy to bear upon a particular convention of patriarchy, demonstrating why it should be destroyed) despite the fact that Mill was uncritically committed to liberal capitalism. Such a practice goes back to the recorded beginning of philosophy, thus generating another pitfall connected to, but also different from, the totalizing annihilationist gesture critiqued in the previous section. By losing itself in itself, by transforming into a practice where philosophers attack each others' theoretical commitments, suggests the annihilation of philosophy itself. That is, we are presented with a particular history called *Philosophy*, based on particular and unexamined "philosophical decisions", that is akin to centuries of attempted annihilations where philosophical "schools" militate against each other, conflated with the theoretical terrains they each attempt to defend over others. I will leave the discussion of this problematic for the next section so that I can establish some general thoughts about philosophy's ability to interpret and clarify in the context of annihilation.

First and foremost we must recognize that philosophy can only demand a terrain or province's annihilation; it cannot, by itself, enact this annihilation. Since the word is grandiose it might seem as if we are attributing to philosophy a power which it otherwise lacks; we thus need to be clear, reasserting previous axioms about the place of philosophical practice. A philosopher cannot literally demolish a theoretical terrain with the power of their thought; a terrain's existence or non existence is based on concrete processes that exist outside of the province of philosophy, though it attempts to intervene, and which draw every philosopher into their orbit. Again, philosophy by its own processes cannot change the world: it intervenes, it clarifies, it attempts to force meaning, it suggests resolutions, some of which are demolitions.

Occasionally, and for very good reason, philosophy can and should suggest the annihilation of a certain body or aspect of theory. While it is correct to also recognize that sometimes such philosophical demands are off-base (that there is even an ongoing struggle amongst various philosophers regarding such a suggestion) this does not mean that such demands should not be made and that, in their historical making, they haven't succeeded in producing the conceptual grounds for a concrete annihilation of theoretical terrains and regions that did indeed require annihilation.

But what about the annihilation of philosophy itself? Claims regarding "the death of philosophy" are not uncommon and are frequently made by those who consider themselves to be scientists free from the taint of philosophy, whatever they imagine this taint to be. Most recently Stephen Hawking claimed that philosophy was an antiquated practice, overtaken by science, and that there was no longer a need for philosophy-as-such.[2] Such claims, however, originate from erroneously defining philosophy according to ontological systemization, assimilationism, and betrayal. Those who proclaim "the death of philosophy" are also those who define philosophy as either one or a combination of the following: i) a speculative ontological system that seeks to be the scaffolding behind science (philosophy masquerading as the science of sciences, a meta-science); ii) a confused liquidation within a particular theoretical terrain (the refusal to think through truth procedures because one is assimilated to a particular sub-terrain/province); iii) attempts to defend an antiquated theoretical terrain in the interests of philosophically preserving the past (betraying truth procedures by forcing them to conform to an a priori logic). What is missed in these proclamations about philosophy's death is that such proclamations are themselves intensely philosophical.

Here it is worth recalling Althusser's claim that scientists often become spontaneous philosophers without realizing it—and I would add, especially when they make proclamations about the state of philosophy. Hawking's statement (and those who have made or will make statements like his) is fundamentally philosophical in that it declares a particular meaning, an interpretative gesture outside of his chosen theoretical terrain, that attempts to force a particular fidelity. Like most expressions of spontaneous philosophy it is logically incoherent: a philosophical claim that philosophy is dead. Claims about the death of philosophy are themselves philosophical interventions. Hawking was not working within his favoured theoretical terrain (physics) but making an interpretative statement that functions outside of, and intervenes upon, the terrain itself, i.e. a philosophical statement. Hence, all arguments about the death of philosophy cannibalize themselves since they are intrinsically philosophical. Physics, mathematics, biology, chemistry, historical materialism, and other theoretical terrains do not make these judgements; they simply produce various truth procedures. Hawking the physicist elaborated physics; to speak about the meaning of physics, let alone his thoughts about philosophy, is to practise philosophy.

Hence philosophy can only be annihilated if thought itself, and consciously thinking about thought (what is woefully short-handed as "critical thinking"), is obliterated. The moment reflection, clarification, and interpretation survive is the same moment in which the kernel of philosophy is preserved.

Annihilating philosophy?

But what should we make of philosophy's apparent attempt to annihilate itself? That is, since the history of philosophy can be read as a history of competing schools of thought, where every school attempts to annihilate another, can we then say that there is such a thing as a purely annihilationist philosophy, i.e. a philosophy that attempts to annihilate philosophy-as-such? Such an option would be different from the vague claims about the "death of philosophy" launched by spontaneous philosophers since it would come from thinkers who are critical of philosophy's history and, due to this critical awareness, might seek to annihilate the terms that make philosophy possible.

Already the history of philosophy seems to be determined by thinkers attempting to demolish the thoughts of other thinkers. Outside observers often imagine that philosophy is a discipline turned upon itself, a specialized world of contested truth that is incapable of historical development. Again we discover that Althusser is correct: although historically conditioned philosophy lacks a history; by itself it simply rephrases the same problems, with its militants lining up to defend these problems, since the days of Parmenides and Heraclitus or even before recorded thought. It is in this context that François Laruelle is interesting as both diagnosis and symptom.

According to Laruelle, the problem with philosophy is that it depends on a prior decision that it cannot fully cognize within its own boundaries. Every philosophy makes a particular "philosophical decision" to structure the world in such a way so as to organize it according to speculative reflection, but remains unaware of this decision; it is thus trapped by the duality wherein "being and thinking are the same".[3] Hence philosophy is "a fundamental pretension and authoritarian legislation over every other thought".[4] Non-philosophy, then, is intended to be the archimedian point capable of unveiling the philosophical decision. More than a meta-philosophy (which would just be philosophy explaining itself according to philosophy), Laruelle attempts to construct a unified theory of philosophy and science; non-philosophy is to philosophy, according to Laruelle, what non-Euclidean geometry is to geometry. Non-philosophy abandons the duality between being and thinking "in order to deduce, not thought, but the transformation of thought from the

Real".[5]

In *Dictionary of Non-Philosophy* Laruelle asserts: "Philosophy is an *a priori* discourse on the one hand with a systematic goal on the other. It posits the world of which being is preformed in the logos with a predicative structure. The predicative structure of philosophical discourse is organized in a speculative reflection."[6] Following from this definition, the "philosophical decision" is "an operation of transcendence which believes...in the possibility of a unitary discourse on Reality. [...] The philosophical Decision [sic] has as a structure the coupling of the Unity of opposites and as a function to hallucinate the One-real and thus to foreclose."[7] And then we have non-philosophy, in response to philosophy and its decision, as "a theory by or according to the One, therefore a unified theory of science and philosophy. It is over time a theoretical, practical and critical discourse, distinct from philosophy without being a meta-philosophy."[8]

What we have here is a diagnosis of the problem of the history of philosophy, a particular apprehension of philosophy-qua-philosophy where *Philosophy* is defined according to prior philosophical decisions that seek to annihilate other philosophical decisions because they do not demonstrate the same dedication to a supposed and foreclosed Real, that is the construct of reality resulting from systems of speculative reflection. Laruelle's non-philosophy is simultaneously an attempt to overstep this history *and* a grand annihilationism that seeks to demolish philosophy-qua-philosophy so as to replace it with his non-philosophy. Laruelle is only partially successful in the overstepping mainly because he recognized the problem of "philosophical decision" caused by a history of assimilationism. He fails to truly demolish philosophy-as-such, thus demonstrating that a philosophical annihilation of philosophy—i.e. a purely anti/non-philosophy— is impossible because it remains precisely within the realm of philosophy. But the attempt is interesting, even when it becomes less interesting when Laruelle, like so many others, spends most of his time courting obscurantism.

Years earlier, when he was first formulating his project of "non-philosophy" in *Philosophy and Non-philosophy*, Laruelle claimed that his project was "one of the solutions that our age must contribute to the problem concerning new writings and new practices of philosophy following the age that came before it".[9] In some ways, this project is laudable in its express attempt to produce "[r]ather than a new philosophy...a new practice of philosophy that detaches it from its own authority and includes within a thought whose origin is wholly other than philosophical... and which is also scientific rather than ontological".[10] And yet this project, at least in its first iteration, is a reinscription rather than rejection of ontological speculation. Already, despite attempts to delineate from the philosophical decision of philosophy-qua-philosophy, we are returned to that realm. As noted previously, the mystification that hampers Laruelle's project undermines his promise of radical popularity.

But this was Laruelle's early period. By the time of that period he calls "Philosophy III", notable for *Principles of Non-philosophy* and *Introduction to Non-Marxism*, we should expect that, based on the claims that he fixed the errors of his past attempts, he transcended the mystical/ontological clutter that undermined his claims about non-philosophy. At this point Laruelle recognizes the obvious problem of his earlier approach:

> philosophy's function is itself divided: it allows science to govern, it says, but pretends to reign over it and, as Principle of Sufficient Philosophy, "posits" the whole of the mix. However, if its unilateralization really affects this very claim or the philosophical authority of the mix, it still can only conserve the two terms and their necessary relation, albeit a new one, such that this unidentification can only equalize them through the materials of a philosophy/science hierarchy *by allowing a reversal of science/philosophy from now on in the*

state of objective appearance bound to the material and projected as support of the new relation.[11]

The point Laruelle is making, once we comb through his opaque syntax, is that philosophy at times does claim to surrender its authority in favour of the authority of science without actually relinquishing philosophical authority (or its "Principle of Sufficient Philosophy", the axiom that the philosophical decision is sufficient and authoritative to legislate the meaning/ interpretation of reality itself). That is, philosophy can easily claim that science is more authoritative than philosophy if at the same time it unilaterally decides the meaning of this relationship, providing a philosophical foundation for the meaning of science so that the transformation of "philosophy/science" into "science/ philosophy" is permitted according to philosophical legislation.

For example, the rise of analytical philosophy (particularly logical positivism) was justified by a recognition of science and maths as being the cornerstones of knowledge; philosophy was conceived as a practice that should be limited according to scientific/mathematical rules. Simultaneously, however, this philosophical practice gave itself a deeper authority by deciding the meaning of science itself. So while it sounded as if philosophy was limiting itself by declaring that science was authoritative and that all questions outside of the rules of science and maths should be banished from philosophical discourse (think Wittgenstein's declaration about "passing over in silence" what could not be spoken about in logical terms, think Ayer's verificationism where questions about "the meaning of life" were in themselves meaningless because they did not accord to a scientific definition of meaning), it was in fact over-bloating its right to decide the meaning of reality (that is, in Laruellian terms, its "philosophical decision") while impoverishing traditional philosophical discourse. Hence we end up with philosophers such as Popper deciding the meaning of science as a whole which, according to Laruelle, would probably be a good example of philosophy reasserting its authority on the sciences while pretending, once these sciences were defined according to a philosophical decision, that philosophy was secondary.

While this is a good diagnosis of a possible problem with philosophy it may also be an impasse in that it relegates all attempts to explain the meaning of theory, particularly scientific theory, to the practice of dubious philosophical decisions. If we are cynical about the practice of philosophy then it might be that we should be cynical about clarification and meaning in general and, if this is the case, Laruelle should just end his project immediately because the most honest "non-philosophy" might have to declare the end of clarification of a given theoretical terrain altogether out of fear of lapsing into the error of philosophical decision. Just let the scientists and mathematicians work things out and refuse a second-order theorization on their business since any type of theorization would be precisely what Laruelle critiques, and what was a problem with *Philosophy and Non-philosophy*: a reassertion of the Principle of Sufficient Philosophy.

Unfortunately Laruelle's solution to this impasse is to embrace speculative ontology and flee back into the realm of the worst kind of philosophy that he has sanctified, thanks to his rarified jargon, as non-philosophy. Although he consistently denies that he is formulating an ontology of this kind the fact is that he is building a formal scaffolding that attempts to legislate meaning *even while simultaneously declaring that philosophy cannot legislate such meaning* by producing a speculative archimedian point. Non-philosophy becomes the legislator of meaning of both science and philosophy simply because it "distinguishes itself from a philosophy or even from a simple science without ceasing to maintain certain precise relations with them".[12] Laruelle invents concepts such as "First Science" and "science-thought" while simultaneously claiming he isn't doing ontology or a first philosophy.

Suspending the speculative jargon—that arcane formal clutter that rushes in to force obscurity—we can reduce Laruelle's project to three characteristics. First: define philosophy, the supposed object of critique, as something that makes up a discursive structure so as to deform reality according to this structure but remains blind to the rules of its operation, a way of thinking that is unaware of how it is being thought. Next: impose a transcendent operation, following the a priori imposition of thought, that believes all reality can be subsumed according to a singular discourse of reflection, banning anything that conflicts with the discursive structure. Finally: propose a foundational theory that exists outside of this "philosophical practice" and name it a "unified theory of science and philosophy" because it is somehow, based on your definition of philosophy, something other than philosophy.

What Laruelle constructs, then, is a system of playing the philosophical game that pretends it is not part of this game by defining it according to its own rarified categories that exclude and obscure participation. Like someone with a gambling addiction who claims they aren't gambling by defining gambling as something that *losers* do and they aren't, according to their subjective understanding, losers. I will define philosophy as x, I will demonstrate the ways in which this x excludes all forms of y, I will imagine the solution z. As long as you are careful to translate all forms of x and y according to the operations of z you can repeat the argument. That is, Laruelle's definition of "philosophy" and its "decision" only make sense if you begin with the conclusion of "non-philosophy" and work your way backwards. There is no argument, no justification for his definitions, only the axiom that non-philosophy is correct and, if it is accepted as correct, then its definition of philosophy and its decision make sense. Non-philosophy is itself a prior decision, an ad hoc position, and it functions by imposing this a priorism on philosophy as a whole—it constructs a particular story of philosophy.

As Brassier has pointed out, Laruelle's non-philosophy is in fact guided by the assumption that philosophy possesses a transhistorical essence—a philosophy-qua-philosophy beyond the general practice I have sketched out in previous chapters—best exemplified by Hegel in that it identifies "philosophy *with* totalization".[13] This "Heideggerian preoccupation with uncovering the essence of philosophy" is an idealist obsession that ignores the fact that philosophy "is an intellectual practice with a complex material history".[14] While it is necessary, as I have argued, to sketch out the general meaning of the practice (i.e. what makes philosophical practice different from scientific practice, the concern of philosophy different from the concern of theory), beyond concrete examples of how this practice is articulated there is no transhistorical philosophical essence. Brassier indicates that to accept that there is such an essence would be similar to accepting that there is an ideal *sport* that lurks beneath the practice of being an athlete and various different sports. Hence:

> when Laruelle declares that "philosophy itself" has told him that it is an auto-affecting whole, one can only respond that "philosophy itself" never speaks, since it is a figment, only philosophers speak—even and especially those philosophers who claim philosophy speaks through them. Far from unmasking philosophy's totalitarian propensities, the assertion that the contingent collection of texts and practices called "philosophy" instantiates an auto-affecting whole, and that those individuals designated as "philosophers" effectuate the system of a universal *cogito* which ventriloquizes its practitioners, actually reiterates the Hegelian idolatry of philosophy which Laruelle claims to subvert. Laruelle ventriloquizes philosophy and then expresses distaste for the

authoritarian pretensions which he has put in its mouth.[15]

Laruelle is thus in fact playing a traditional philosophical game. By constructing his own speculative system that tells a particular story about philosophy, reducing it to his own language, he is doing precisely what the kind of philosopher he treats as representative of philosophy as a whole (i.e. Hegel) has done: incorporating the movement of all thinking into his discourse, interpreting and deforming it according to his own prior decision, and legislating against anything that troubles these categories. For Hegel also thought that he could translate every philosophical endeavour according to his system, demonstrating why they were incomplete and part of a total, unfolding process; he proposed a categorical language, a grammar, that slotted all prior thought forms into his theology; he imagined he was proposing a science of reality. Laruelle, who also proposes a science of reality, possesses his own ontological grammar, though he claims he's not an ontologist: the Real instead of the Absolute, the One instead of the Idea. Even if he calls his project "non-philosophy" he is doing no less than what the ontologist—the philosopher-qua-philosopher—has been doing since Plato: providing a cartography or reality and legislating against all thought that threatens this cartography. He is another speculative system builder, the very definition of the philosopher regardless of his *non*-syntax.

The tradition of Marxism, however, has been uncomfortable with speculative systems. Laruelle is aware of this: in the act of proposing the category of non-philosophy his attention must necessarily turn to the tradition that, around 8 decades earlier, washed its hands of philosophy-as-such. Since Marxism declared itself done with philosophy, Laruelle, who declares the same, must find a reason to justify his project against a Marxist grain that might dismiss it as part of the same problem. Hence, Laruelle approaches Marxism with the same rationale that he extended to philosophy as a whole: Marxism is a particular variant of philosophy, though it struggles to claim the terrain of science, and so must be grounded according to a non-philosophical elaboration of its theoretical concerns, i.e. non-Marxism.

Whereas in the previous chapter we treated Laruelle as paradigmatic of an insufficient demystifying practice of philosophy—a reification of all the problems with pre-Marxist philosophy despite its express attempts to overcome these problems—here we can treat this same project as a failed but notable attempt at annihilation that will tell us something about philosophy in general, as well as the innumerable and often misguided declarations of "the death [or at least the end] of philosophy". On the one hand he provides an interesting diagnosis of a particular problem of the history of philosophical practice, the fidelity to the prior philosophical decision that results in a hermetically sealed echo chamber of thought divided amongst various thought sects. On the other hand, rather than demystifying this problem—that is, by setting philosophy back on its feet by figuring out what it is actually operating beneath traditional philosophical vanity (the simple practice of intervention, of clarification and forcing meaning)—he remystifies it according to his totalizing meta-ontology of non-philosophy, an ontology of ontologies based upon an idealization of philosophy and a subtraction of his own philosophy from this idealization.

We do not have to look very hard to discover proof that Laruelle has been reabsorbed into the classical, pre-materialist philosophy he desires to critique. Throughout *Principles of Non-philosophy* (and to a lesser extent *Introduction to Non-Marxism*) Laruelle obsesses over the divide between philosophies of "transcendence" (i.e. Kant) and philosophies of "immanence" (i.e. Spinoza). He correctly notes these are prior philosophical decisions that should be overstepped but then, like Hegel before him, creates a system that can account for both. (Of course,

Laruelle attempts to distance himself from Hegel by submitting the Hegelian system to the same critique of philosophical decision and thus seems to align with Feuerbach, but unlike Feuerbach his non-philosophy becomes another speculative system as ontologically speculative as Hegel's. In this sense Laruelle is a strange hybrid of Feuerbach and Hegel, and his occasional mentions of Feuerbach[16] might be proof of a guilty conscience.) In order to truly escape the boundaries of the pre-materialist philosophical past, however, we need to reject the ontological significance of "transcendence" and "immanence"; these are ultimately idealist terms, ciphers of a philosophy that has not passed under the shadow of the eleventh thesis, because they are philosophical decisions about the hidden scaffolding of reality—they are speculative/idealist *theory*, the point where philosophy becomes theology.

As Esteve Morera writes in his seminal work on Gramsci:

> care must be taken to interpret the meaning of fundamental terms such as 'immanence' and 'transcendence'. These terms have long standing in philosophical writings; Gramsci uses them in his philosophical analysis of historical materialism. Because these terms are laden with philosophical content that is often extraneous to Marxism, there is the possibility of carrying those contents into Gramsci's reconstruction of Marxism, thus giving rise to Husserlian variations, Crocean variations, etc. [...] [W]ords are often used in a metaphorical sense, metaphorical because, although the word is the same, the concept is not.[17]

What Morera is indicating in the above passage is the ways in which terms like "transcendence" and "immanence" are alien to a philosophy that has emerged from the shadow of Marx's eleventh thesis, such as Gramsci's work. Of course, some of the same names carry over but they no longer possess the same import since we are now dealing with a philosophical practice that rejects ontology-qua-ontology as "extraneous". There are of course interlocutors who cannot help but continue to treat these names with the older conceptual significance. For Morera these are the people who force this significance upon Gramsci just as Laruelle forces the same significance upon thought itself. The general point, here, is that philosophies of immanence or transcendence are as immaterial as debates about the secret nature of God.

Hence with Laruelle we encounter an attempt to annihilate philosophy-as-such and, following this attempted annihilation, the aim to build a new philosophical (or "non-philosophical") project upon these demolished ruins. Those treated as the key philosophers of modernity and "post-modernity" due to their supposed ontological particularity—Kant, Hegel, Nietzsche, Husserl, Heidegger, Wittgenstein, Levinas, Derrida, Deleuze— are singled out as obstacles to be overcome, particular instances that define philosophy as a whole...ciphers of problems that stretch back to the competing projects of Heraclitus and Parmenides. For through these ontological ciphers the whole of philosophy is understood as functioning as a terrain, as if it possesses a theoretical coherence with the proper name *Philosophy*, and in order to overcome the problems of this supposed terrain (being, destiny, reason, necessity, immanence, transcendence, etc.) a grand act of annihilation and reconstitution is in order.

There is something laudable about Laruelle's project that every radical philosophical practice can and should take into account. After all, if we are to chart the course of many so-called "contintental" thinkers from Hegel to Badiou,[18] as long as we find a way to reinterpret and scuttle Marxist philosophical traditions within this account, we will discover a problematic that may indeed be worthy of annihilation. Whether or not Laruelle's proposed demolition errs on the side of homogenization (i.e. his placement of the more material problematic of "necessity" alongside the ontological concern of "being" is a category mistake), at the very least he is attempting to do away with a landscape that has become decadent. Indeed Nietzsche failed to understand the precise meaning of this decadence, despite his complaints against its existence and supposed origin, because he himself was invested in its foundational fact.

The problem I have been trying to elucidate, however, is that Laruelle's project is one that is turned upon itself so that it becomes a project of annihilating the very basis upon which annihilatory judgements can be made. When he critiques the prior "philosophical decision" he does so by forcing his own philosophical decision. Such a tendency demonstrates an inability to understand what philosophy *is* beneath its historically conditioned appearance, especially the clear understanding of its meaning produced by the emergence of the Marxist terrain. Of course, philosophy is that which is capable of taking itself as its own object of thought—and thus partially treating itself as a terrain that requires clarification—but Laruelle's project of non-philosophy attempts to annihilate philosophy in the very act of performing philosophy, hence his refusal to determine his theory according to the category of meta-philosophy.[19] Such an attempt is a problem not because of its apparent pragmatic limitations (after all, to annihilate philosophy by performing philosophical gestures seems, at first glance, rather self-defeating and, to his credit, Laruelle warns against this "nihilistic" interpretation of non-philosophy), since philosophers are usually not dissuaded by such limitations, but because it fails to understand that philosophy's root significance is in this act of performance (i.e. the practice of forcing clarity) and that philosophy is not, even if sometimes treated as such, a theoretical terrain.

Thus by presupposing a theoretical terrain that is philosophy rather than understanding that the history of philosophy is simply a series of gestures that, lacking their own intrinsic and unified history, are a complex and varied expression of its interaction with the history of theory, Laruelle's project of annihilation is aimed at something he himself has invented by constructing, as discussed in the previous chapter, a pseudo-history of philosophy. Philosophy, according to Laruelle, is that terrain which takes itself as sufficient/necessary for reality, coding/decoding/recoding language and thought according to this demand. But philosophy is not that which, as discussed from the outset of this book, can or should be theoretically consistent in the first place, though it may indeed demand, in the interest of clarity, that a theoretical terrain demonstrates consistency. Therefore, according to his own definition, Laruelle's entire project begins by confusing philosophy with theory and thus seeks a fantastical coherence that, once assembled from those thinkers and ontological debates that best demonstrate this invented coherence, can be presented as the essence of philosophy as a whole. From this complex suturing, Laruelle is in the position to declare the annihilation of that which does not exist precisely in the way he imagines it exists.

Any problems with philosophy that the Laruellian project names are, if significant problems at all,[20] merely symptoms that philosophical practice has and will continue to encounter. These symptoms are not due to the disease of philosophy since philosophy lacks the significance, historical coherence, or theoretical strength to be such a disease. Rather, this disease is the result of ideological commitments inherited from those theoretical terrains that may indeed require annihilation. (In some ways Nietzsche better understood the root of the problem than Laruelle: he grasped that the sickness of philosophy was due to the ideology produced by real-world events; he simply targeted the wrong origins and suspects, unaware that he was also suffering from the malady he was incapable of diagnosing.) Nor is there only one disease, one grand suspect for all of the bad routes philosophy has taken, because every historical conjuncture will present new ideological problems while simultaneously transforming those problems that continue to persist.

Ultimately, the Laruellian project may be *assimilationist* in that, by treating philosophy as a theoretical terrain, it assimilates itself to a particular understanding of the importance of philosophy that we have already transgressed. "Non-philosophy is the only usage of philosophy that is not programmed by it," Laruelle writes: "Then by whom or what is it programmed? [...] [U]ltimately by 'science' rather than philosophy."[21] And yet this claim about non-philosophy is in fact the very definition of philosophy, and one that Laruelle should have been aware of, that we already possess. Philosophy is not ultimately "programmed" by philosophy but by other theoretical terrains and most importantly—if we are to be conscious of this programming and our theoretical commitment—it is programmed by scientific terrains. Lacking a history, and as Althusser with all his problems taught us, every philosophy is called into being by scientific truth procedures.

So what precisely does this examination of Laruelle's project teach us? That philosophy is incapable of annihilating itself because, aside from the impossibility of total auto-cannibalism (i.e. one would die before completely consuming oneself), which Laruelle in fact bans, it lacks a history and theoretical coherence to be annihilated in the first place. There is no philosophy-qua-philosophy, no philosophy-as such, only instances of philosophizing united by a very general way of doing thought. A practice is not that which can be annihilated, especially if you are practising it while proclaiming annihilation, it is simply practised or not practised...And Laruelle is practising philosophy, exhibiting the only thing that philosophy actually *is*, while naming it *non-philosophy*. The only thing that makes this project non-philosophical—and non-philosophical in the pejorative sense—is that it fails to produce significant clarity.

The annihilationist demand

When philosophy causes us to consider the necessity of annihilating a particular terrain or province, and forces this consideration while avoiding the pitfalls of betrayal and assimilation, we are presented with the starkest example of class struggle in the realm of theory. Usually the stakes behind this annihilationist demand are high; to suggest the demolition of a terrain is to simultaneously attempt to force the recognition that a particular theoretical tendency hinders existence. Most importantly, annihilationist gestures that do not go awry (as the Nietzschean and Laruellian projects went awry) receive their strength from those concrete and mass struggles that surround these rarified struggles in thought.

Take, for example, those philosophers who placed themselves in service of the concrete struggle against modern slavery by demanding the amelioration of every theoretical terrain and province that generated pseudo-truth procedures dedicated to the moral, religious, economic, and scientific justification of this social-historical edifice. Entire theoretical structures were singled out for liquidation; their potential clarity was no longer at issue, the clarity of choice had been established earlier and, on the basis of this clarity, the role of the radical philosophical militant was to storm the gates of these racist heavens and subject their sacred truths to the conceptual guillotine. While it might have made sense in an earlier moment of philosophical struggle to demonstrate, through the practice of forcing clarity, that a theoretical corpus such as physiognomy was not consistent with the truth procedures of biological theory as a whole, the mass struggle in the concrete world would eventually push the struggle in the realm of thought into a necessarily narrower function, sharper because of its narrowness: the utter obliteration of these backward terrains based on the justification of the struggle itself rather than an appeal to a terrain's overall meaning.

At these moments, where the truth procedure of history possessed the power to overdetermine the interior procedures of a given terrain, we discover philosophers dedicated to the stakes of these struggle no longer arguing for the quality of a given sub-terrain's truth value according to the overall terrain's logic; instead, this annihilationist forcing is placed in service of the larger struggle: the people are rising up, they are proving by their actions and demands that they are human, they are relegating all claims that it could be otherwise to the past...any theory that would claim otherwise should not be dismissed because it fails to satisfy the truth requirements of its larger terrain, its dismissal is due to the fact that its existence contradicts the real movement of living people, that is existence as a whole.

Hence the difference between John Hepburn's attempt to prove that anti-slavery was a superior Christian ethics in 1715 and the statements made by John Brown in 1859 during his execution for leading a slave rebellion. The former labours to prove that abolition is consistent with the Golden Rule; the latter has already accepted that this is a fact and demands the annihilation of any aspect of his religion that would claim otherwise: "to have interfered as I have done...in behalf of [God's] despised poor, was not wrong, but right". The historical conjuncture was different; Brown was part of an emergent mass movement that would allow for the possibility of an annihilationist practice. We can go further and investigate the gap between the New Afrikan abolitionists: whereas Frederick Douglass worked hard to prove that the African slave was a human being, Malcolm X's militancy in thought, parallel to his militancy in concrete action, already understood this assumption as a priori and thus treated any theory that would say otherwise as meaningless.

Therefore, there is a process wherein the practice of forcing clarity becomes the practice of annihilation, and where the latter receives its strength from the work of the former, that should teach us something about philosophical practice in general.

For there are times when a theoretical terrain or province will emerge that, due to a history where multiple acts of clarifying interventions have already taken place, ought to be treated as destined for annihilation. Sometimes it is useless to return to mapping an enemy terrain so as to force a clarity in choice when past mappings have already foreclosed on this terrain's very existence.

So when we are faced with the emergence of theories such as, for example, evolutionary psychology and other bio-determinist nonsense, it might be bad philosophical practice to waste time demonstrating through argument why these repellant ideologies are "bad science" and thus inconsistent with the scientific terrains in which they manifest. Such a clarification was already performed before historical struggles delegitimated scientific racism; the philosophical interventions designed to demonstrate the erroneousness of phrenology and physiognomy should have already provided us with the foundation to begin our intervention by demanding the destruction of these contemporary variants of past mistakes. It may be a despicable act of bad faith, then, to treat these dismal echoes of past mistakes as worthy of philosophical consideration. Rather, philosophy demands their obliteration.

From annihilation to transformation

The aphorism with which Marx begins *The 18th Brumaire of Louis Bonaparte*, that history repeats itself first as tragedy and secondly as farce,[22] might imply something significant about the practice of philosophical annihilation. The occasional repetition of history often locates itself in conceptual procedures where the same questions, linked to unsolved historical dilemmas, are reflected within a given theoretical terrain. Earlier I discussed the repetition of racial science (where the errors of phrenology are repeated in the contemporary errors of evolutionary psychology), but this is only one example. If we are also, as Marx goes on to say in the same passage, hampered by the weight of dead generations, then every theoretical terrain will find itself overburdened by its history and discover either a tragic or farcical repetition of those problems it has already, though in different provincial forms, overcome.

The fact that the problem of "revisionism" continues to hamper the terrain of historical materialism is a salient example of this repetition. Since Eduard Bernstein, this terrain has experienced the resurgence of a reformist ideology that has sought to subsume the dynamic of class struggle—the terrain's overall logic of development—in the practice of bourgeois legality. It repeated itself when it was rebranded, by Khrushchev, as "peaceful co-existence with capitalism"; it was rebranded again, though without cynicism or opportunistic betrayal, in Allende's Chile where socialism was "won" through peaceful elections without, for all that, destroying the institutions of class power that would enable Pinochet's coup; it manifests in every remaining revisionist communist party that is a legal electoral entity in bourgeois democracies, promising socialism through the ballot box.

Another example: the contemporary "movementist" strategy of anti-capitalism, derived from the "Arab Spring" and "the Movement of the Squares" and "Occupy", that is simply a repetition of the anti-globalization movement and, before that, multiple sites of anarchist struggle. Such an approach to revolutionary strategy barely counts as a theoretical terrain due to the simplicity of its topography. Here, perhaps, we are confronted with a geographic wasteland that requires abandonment. After all, when we are faced with a repetition that has never succeeded in establishing anything beyond the reiteration of failure then it makes no sense to continue clarifying an absence.[23]

One more example: those revolutionary organizations that simply wish to formulaically repeat the experience of the Russian or Chinese Revolutions—an intentional repetition of failure because such organizations, if they were to proclaim unquestioned fidelity to these experiences, would have to develop an account of history that, against the evidence, would prove that these failed movements were not failures. The trick is to grasp the successes as well as the failures and clarify the theoretical terrain in light of the former rather than the latter. Instead the desire to dogmatically imitate an experience results in some communist organizations farcically resembling historical reenactment societies.

Thus we are often presented with a general continuum between tragedy and farce. Due to the proven erroneous nature of a particular theory or interior development, annihilation is required so that we are not caught in an endless recurrence of farce. For the historic problem of revisionism has indeed become farcical at the point where self-proclaimed socialist organizations consistently locate their strategy in the practice of bourgeois electoral politics, or when the movementist strategy produces yet another #occupy, or when the legacy of Stalin is promoted as a simple and uncritical formula for party politics, or when innumerable Trotskyist sects promise the same "alternative" dogmatism they have promised for decades.

To demand the annihilation of these theoretical regions is a necessary part of any philosophical struggle that is capable of forcing us to consider a new return to what has been established, through class struggle, in the terrain of historical materialism. A clearing of the historical clutter so that the ruins of the past can finally be buried—this is what we need to suggest—and we can focus on the possibility of that theoretical rupture which is also in continuity with the terrain as a whole.

The problem, however, is that philosophy can only demand such an annihilation—can hope to force its possibility by suggesting the need to demolish those repetitive aspects of the past that continue to haunt the terrain—and is not itself that which can bring annihilation. After all, past philosophical struggles have already attempted to force such annihilating moments, and have indeed provided arguments that should have convinced us that this was the proper course of action, but, for all that, so many attempted annihilations have failed to become total.

Moreover, philosophy as a whole, right at the moment when it claims it is involved in annihilation, often tends to incorporate the haunted past that may have been annihilated in a given theoretical terrain within itself. For example, Engels' theoretical struggle against Eugen Duhring was successful in leading to the annihilation of Duhring's philosophy from the terrain of historical materialism to the extent that no one even speaks Duhring's name except in reference to a failed thinker who was rendered obsolete by Engels' intervention. And yet Duhring's discredited theory found its way into post-modern philosophy and its preoccupation with an abstract notion of power—the very basis of Duhring's theory.

Hence, when philosophy is not aware of itself and its relation to class struggle in a visceral sense, it finds itself acting according to various theoretical dead-ends that should have been immolated on history's funeral pyre. Again we must recognize the importance of Althusser who, in declaring that philosophy lacked its own history, understood that philosophy was that discipline that was capable of repeating historical errors at the very moment it was claiming to critique historical moments. Back to Plato, back to Aristotle, back to Kant and Hegel! Not that we should forget this past, or that these long dead thinkers have nothing to say about the present, only that "just as [we] seem to be occupied with revolutionizing [our]selves and things, creating something that did not exist before...[we] anxiously conjure up the spirits of the past".[24] Thus, we must keep demanding the annihilation of what has already been annihilated and be wary of what traditions are mobilized in these demands if we are to be philosophically honest.

Philosophical annihilation can never be total, at least not until the possibility of communism is finally (if ever) realized and the absence of classes prevents the recurrence of every error that was dependent on the situation of social class. It is a demand, not a procedure that can actually be affected by philosophy itself...And though annihilation is an important demand, it is far less important than the demand to which it is connected: the demand for transformation.

Notes

1. Horkheimer and Adorno, *Dialectic of Enlightenment*, 81-119.
2. See, for example, https://philosophynow.org/issues/82/Hawking_contra_Philosophy.
3. Laruelle, *Introduction to Non-Marxism*, 23.
4. Ibid., 165.
5. Ibid., 23.
6. Laruelle, *Dictionary of Non-Philosophy*, 57.
7. Ibid., 56.
8. Ibid., 45.
9. Laruelle, *Philosophy and Non-Philosophy*, 5.
10. Ibid., 1.
11. Laruelle, *Principles of Non-philosophy*, 54.
12. Ibid., 37.
13. Brassier, 131.
14. Ibid., 133.
15. Ibid., 133-134.
16. Laruelle, *Principles of Non-philosophy*, 83, 88.
17. Morera, *Gramsci's Historicism*, 4.
18. Although, to be fair, Badiou (along with his students such as Meillassoux) attempts to bridge the gap between the "continental" and "analytical" traditions.
19. Ibid., 9-10.
20. Often Laruelle's project of "non-philosophy" resembles the far less interesting, erroneous and inaccurate, and even

comical project of Korzybski's "general semantics" where all the sins of thought were attributed to some Aristotelian conspiracy—a project that, in its grand assumptions about what Aristotle's philosophy meant and its supposed influence in thought, possessed far more teleological force than Aristotle's own understanding of teleology. We should not, to be fair, confuse a sophisticated thinker such as Laruelle with a hack pop-philosopher such as Korzybski even if there are troubling points of intersection.

21. Laruelle, *Philosophy and Non-philosophy*, 10.
22. Marx, *18th Brumaire*, 15.
23. For a further examination of movementism see my book *The Communist Necessity* (Montreal: Kersplebedeb, 2014).
24. Marx, *18th Brumaire*, 15.

Chapter Seven

philosophy and transformation

...the world we have most intimately known, the world in which we feel 'safe' (even if such feelings are based on illusions), must be radically changed. Perhaps it is the knowledge that everyone must change, not just those we label enemies or oppressors, that has so far served to check our revolutionary impulses. Those revolutionary impulses must freely inform our theory and practice...if we are to transform our present reality.

bell hooks, Feminist Theory: from margins to center

In the first chapter, when I listed the five propositions that would guide this treatise's discussion, I concluded with the proposition that philosophy does not by itself produce change (in the sense of historical motion, or history in itself) but that any "changing of the world" is, in the final instance, the result of concrete practice. None of this is to say that philosophical practice does not have a role in clarifying the choices that may need to be made in the realm of concrete practice, only that when we claim, as Marx does, that "philosophy only interprets the world but the point is to change it", we do not accidentally make the category mistake of confusing interpretation with transformation.

Indeed, philosophers have historically tended to make such a confusion. Sometimes they mistake, as discussed earlier, philosophy with theory—but this is a rather grand mistake, one that is not made by those philosophers who consider themselves logical and pragmatic. Even without making this mistake, however, the confusion persists: there is a tendency, on the part of many philosophers, to imagine that social change is accomplished primarily through the business of making air-tight arguments, as if history's motion is derived from rational debate rather than class struggle.

Take, for example, the significance Mill accorded to an open society of free expression, what others would call "the marketplace of ideas", where liberalized and rational debate would promote social change: according to this "invisible hand" logic, bad/irrational ideas would eventually disappear or, if they did linger, they would remain as ineffective and amusing anachronisms useful for teaching citizens about past ignorance. Is it any wonder that those who are devoted to this conception of reality are led to believe that Mill's arguments about women's suffrage were the motive force behind the success of this political struggle and not, as history should teach us, a mass movement of women who, by their actions, forced social change? While we cannot deny that the arguments of Mill and others were useful in supporting such a transformative movement, to assume that the transformation was simply the result of rational debate—especially when the oppressor is insensible to the rationality of the oppressed—is to treat the practice of philosophy with more significance than it deserves.

As I have already noted, though they are indeed useful in developing an anti-capitalist way of thinking and functioning as intellectual weapons for radicals, philosophical arguments will not convince the ruling class to abdicate the historical stage. There have been successive philosophical assaults on the edifice of bourgeois reason that have not succeeded in changing the world. The ruling classes are quite capable of finding their own philosophers, just as they are capable of locking political debate within the confines of their ideology.

One way of escaping the above problem and making sense of the apparent contradiction between interpretation and transformation is to read the eleventh thesis alongside Lenin's well-known claim that "without revolutionary theory there can be no revolutionary movement". After all, to misread the Leninist qualification as a demand for the primacy of philosophy—for focusing primarily on the interpretive gesture—will result in a grave error. For Lenin is speaking of theory, not philosophy, and theory is always that which develops its truth procedure according to a particular and concrete practice. Philosophical practice lurks at a more abstract level; it may demand theoretical training but it is not, in itself, this training.

In this sense, all of the dictums devoted to flipping the eleventh thesis—Adorno's *Negative Dialectics*, the odd statement made by popular thinkers such as Zizek—where we are encouraged to treat the interpretive gesture as fundamental, or even as change in itself, misconstrue the universality we can attribute to Marx's statement. Following the demystification of the world, following the rupture from an ethos that confused philosophy with theory, we cannot pretend as if philosophical practice is revolutionary in and by itself. After all, without the existence of theoretical terrains brought into being by concrete struggles there would be nothing to interpret.

And yet the Leninist exhortation regarding theory and practice was, in some ways, a philosophical intervention in that it was a statement clarifying theory's relation to practice designed to demarcate the grounds upon which action is dependent. That is to say, while philosophy in and of itself cannot and should not be confused with theory and/or praxis, it does find its place in that abstracted moment that attempts to force a decision regarding theory and activity. To abandon "changing the world" so as to go back to the business of "interpreting the world" (thus imagining that a return to the latter will result in a new practice of the former), is the result of bad binary thinking that would have us interpret the eleventh thesis as a conditional argument: if the world is properly interpreted, then it can be changed. But the world *is* being interpreted, and has been interpreted, and the point is to understand how this act of interpretation lurks alongside transformation and, in this lurking, may be placed in the service of change.

It is not as if we have reached an epoch where all interpretation has ceased and anti-capitalists are engaged in struggle without bothering to reflect on the meaning of their struggle (though, admittedly, a lack of reflection is still widespread). While it is true that there are indeed many people who are rebelling against the current state of affairs without thinking deeply about what this rebellion means, or what they are even concretely fighting for, there are also many critical academics who argue for an abdication of struggle and entreat us to return to the act of interpretation. How can we return to a practice many of us have never succeeded, or may never succeed, in escaping?

Disdain

To be fair, the desire to privilege a practice of interpreting the world is perhaps a response to the anti-intellectualism promoted by those who would prefer action at the expense of thinking. After all, if and when a philosophical intervention calls a terrain or province into question—thus forcing those invested in this region to question the truth value of their commitments—it is often easier to banish such interventions and foreclose on thought.

When we investigate the world, and attempt to intervene upon a terrain in which those committed to this terrain are active in pursuing various articulations of its truth procedure, the act of forcing clarity or demanding annihilation will often encounter, rightly or wrongly, scorn. For example, those militantly committed to a given theory will not appreciate an intervention that forces them to reconsider its efficacy. At the same time, however, there are often good reasons to resist such an intervention because there have been so many times when these interventions have indeed been off-base, betrayed by their own erroneous theoretical commitments. Once again we need to recognize that the practice of philosophy is not foundational; its only authority is in its ability to force meaning, demanding clarity or annihilation, and because it is always in service to a theoretical terrain it can always fail in its aim.

Of course, those philosophers who do not want to accept their proper place are always offended by those who would see them banished from their republic, side-lined by the movements and practices upon which they would wish to declare meaning. Thus, in a context where the practice of philosophy is being marginalized, it makes sense that the philosopher would argue for a total focus on interpretation and, in this argument, attempt to make themself central to the unfolding of a given truth procedure. Karl Popper's project regarding the meaning of science makes sense in this context: all of its attempts to provide a speculative basis to scientific terrains—to reverse the relationship between theory and philosophy so that philosophy could make itself the foundation of scientific reason—were perhaps the result of the average scientist's disdain for (if not blithe dismissal of) Popper's thoughts on the matter.[1]

Despite these misguided demands to return to the practice of investigation, we should at least recognize that there is a disdain for thought that often helps generate, because of its anti-intellectualism, the contrary demand to return to the interpretative gesture. But this disdain is often and also a disdain for theory which forgets, due to its myopic focus on practice, that every practice is also conditioned by a theoretical terrain. While every terrain is only brought into existence and developed through concrete practices, our interactions with the world are also conditioned by the terrains that we (as a species) have produced—and when we forget that this is the case we may be in danger of affecting a given terrain with our mistaken and unreflective actions.

After all, the artist who scorns the terrain of art theory because they believe that their practice of art is more important than the practices of innumerable artists who have allowed for the unfolding of artistic theory (that is, the theoretical establishment about what art has been, what it is now, and what it will become, based on the truth procedure of producing art within a historical succession of previous artistic productions) will probably produce work that is ignorant of its historical placement, of its possible originality, of what it *is* in the context of innumerable expressions that are the grounds for declaring the meaning of any and every artistic practice. Here I am reminded of a gallery showing that included artists whose work was derivative of Duchamp's ready-mades but, because of their disdain for history and theory, were arrogantly certain that they were producing conceptually original work. What would happen to the terrain of artistic theory if we were to treat such a gallery showing as foundational? Its history would become meaningless; we would be doomed to repeat the same artistic practices ad infinitum. So at some level we do accept the primacy of the truth procedure that accrues, through practice, within a theoretical terrain, even if it is often threatened.

It is worth noting, again, the primacy of the scientific terrain. While the theoretical terrain of visual art, for example, may be occasionally threatened by some level of wilful amnesia and disrespect of past practices, it is much more difficult, though not impossible, to make the same error with the sciences. That is, it is difficult to imagine a physicist demonstrating in practice an utter disdain for the current paradigm by going back to the problematics of the Newtonian paradigm and asserting an alternate version of its theory of gravity. While it is not impossible that such a physicist exists, it is doubtful that their labour would produce anything scientifically salient.

In any case, the interpretive gesture is often sacrificed upon an altar of practice that disdains thought—and if it disdains theory, despite being unconsciously invested in theory, then it definitely disdains philosophy. Therefore, at these moments, philosophical intervention becomes necessary so as to challenge a possible catastrophe.

Spontaneity and catastrophe

Catastrophe becomes imminent when the militants of a particular terrain encounter, upon discovering interior contradictions and choices, a spontaneous philosophy generated by their desire to make sense of the world in which they're ensconced. Encountering temporary limits in a terrain demands explanation; myriad explanations and internal interventions will be auto-generated to make sense of crisis. Unfortunately, the majority of these spontaneous philosophies are interventions that will be guilty of betrayal or assimilation due to their inability to grasp the unquestioned political commitments from which they emerge.

In the fourth chapter I discussed the ways in which those involved in developing a given terrain's various theoretical concerns often find themselves unconsciously and spontaneously practising philosophy. I argued that a failure to recognize one's shift from theory into philosophy could lead to a confusion of the latter with the former and thus a failure to generate clarity. Such a confusion is what may result in catastrophe, though it sometimes happens in ways that may appear at first to be rather banal. Such a banality, though, might still reify the "common sense" ideology of the current conjuncture.

Take, for example, a situation where artists and curators who, upon encountering the rule of austerity and the limits of a model of government funding, decide that the solution is to embrace the logic of neo-liberalization, accepting as *fait accompli* an end to public arts funding.[2] Here is a spontaneous intervention that possesses significant theoretical and practical ramifications; it is an intervention that implies that the practice of art should be bound to a purer logic of capitalism. Moreover, it is an intervention that attempts to force a decision about the meaning of art: the logic of the commodity should be the truth procedure of these theoretical terrains. Positivism, a return to pure formalism, an elevation to the status of immanent truth value of *art for art's sake*—which is to say, art for the sake of the ruling class.

The reason why these spontaneous philosophical interventions, from the simplest to the most complex, almost always end up reifying some variant of ruling class ideology is because this is the general problem of spontaneity. That is, the assumption that a radical theory and practice will emerge from the spontaneous practices of the masses in general (the dogma of movementist politics) has been disproven by innumerable historical events: in actual fact, spontaneous rebellions that were not theoretically and practically structured by an intervening and unified organization have always ended up reasserting a state of affairs that falls somewhere along the spectrum of ruling class ideology—from social democracy to outright fascism. This is because the various camps of the ruling class are already organized and their values, due to this hegemony, are the most compelling. Lenin's argument for a revolutionary vanguard organization was justified on this basis.

Hence, it is useful to think of the practice of philosophy as a metaphorically Leninist practice. This is not to say that the dedicated philosopher who intervenes in a non-spontaneous manner upon a given theoretical terrain will necessarily be a Leninist in the political-theoretical meaning of the term, only that they will intervene coherently and reflectively from a hypothetical outside point. This hypothetical outside will of course be conditioned by various political, ethical, and theoretical commitments, but if it recognizes its conditioning it will also recognize what is at stake and not make the same errors as those spontaneous philosophical interventions that are most often incapable of reflection.

To practise philosophy consciously and rigorously should mean to struggle against all forms of spontaneous philosophizing that exist, because of their spontaneity, to force a meaning that was already conditioned and declared by ruling class ideology.

We know that the great philosophers of the past treated opinion and baseless belief as distinct from, if not opposed to, knowledge. They understood that a catastrophe in thought resulted from a practice that granted the status of truth to the realm of opinion. And though, since it is incapable of concretely changing the world, it is impossible for philosophy by itself to prevent catastrophe, it can at least work against any possible spontaneous justification—this forcing of a concrete catastrophe that will code and recode various theoretical terrains with its apocalypse—in the hope that its intervention will provide the clarity, or even the demand for annihilation, necessary to justify any and every counter-movement.

Tailism and adventurism

Although the practice of philosophy should not be confused with those practices that are intimately connected with transformation, it will hopefully be clear that philosophy should in some way, though interpretive, have a role to play in any radical changing of the world. In the service of, or opposed to, those social movements that cannot help but generate theory in their concrete practices, a radical philosophical practice can and should investigate and intervene in the realm of thought so as to make the process of transformation clear. At times, philosophy will necessarily tail these transformative movements and attempt to clarify and map an unfolding terrain. At other times, philosophy will venture out into the void wherein a new terrain has not yet emerged and, despite its ignorance of what will be brought into being, demand a transformation that it itself is incapable of producing.

Hence, the practice of philosophy is either tailist or adventurist. While these qualifications might be political and theoretical errors in other contexts, they are simply the fact of philosophical practice. Philosophy will never, by itself, be as historically and socially relevant as the social practice and theory that can avoid these errors while also possessing the power to actually change the world.

Philosophy lags behind because it lacks the power to lead anything other than itself; it is led by the theoretical geography called into being by those movements that will also produce their own philosophers. Presented with a terrain conjured into existence by the radical practices of those movements to which they have tied themselves, this paradigmatic philosophical practice was understood long ago by Hegel in that famous passage from the preface of the *Philosophy of Right*:

> A further word on *issuing instructions* on how the world ought to be: philosophy, at any rate, always comes too late to perform this function. As the *thought* of the world, it appears only at the time when actuality has gone through its formative process and attained its completed state. [...] When philosophy paints its grey in grey, a shape of life has grown from the old, and it cannot be rejuvenated but only recognized, by the grey in grey of philosophy; the owl of Minerva, takes its flight only with the onset of dusk.[3]

Here philosophy does come too late, at the dusk of the already emergent terrain, the completion of reality's continuous formation, made ready for intervention.

Philosophy also adventures out into those empty spaces that it cannot establish. Such adventures are either an attempt to call for further theoretical development or, the deeper into this vacuum they roam, confused moments of utopian speculation. And though such a philosophical practice may indeed violate Wittgenstein's closing comments in the *Tractatus*, it is significant insofar as it promotes the necessity of transformation. Here the philosopher loses themself in the void in the hope that they will be found by that movement which will transform this abyss into a substantial geography and, in doing so, permit them to again speak with authority. Of course, when such adventures lead so far into these distant regions that they become lost in utopianism, it is unclear whether or not they will ever be found by those movements they have outpaced—so distant from a potential geography, they may become irrevocably lost in an abyss that has swallowed their own mapping. The socialist movements of the nineteenth century never found Saint-Simon and Fourier since the theoretical terrains they produced were not those that these utopians had imagined. Even still, and as Marx and Engels would admit, Saint-Simon and Fourier's adventurism encouraged the emergence of this terrain.

In both of these cases, however, philosophy does possess some relation, however limited, to the practice of changing the world: it may clarify and justify this transformation (perhaps even going so far as to suggest the annihilation of those provinces and terrains that conflict with this transformation); it may attempt to make the necessity of this transformation clear. Hence, philosophy potentially aids transformation in the clarity it can generate as well as in its practice of forcing choice, demanding the necessity of transformation. While such a role is far from world historical, and while the practice of interpretation should not be mistaken for the practice of transformation, we should at least recognize that a philosophy driven by the logic of transformation may indeed, if it does not lose itself completely in an adventurist practice, be significant. Hence, if philosophy is to be significant then herein is where its significance lies.

In the shadow of the eleventh thesis

Philosophy has been irrevocably altered since Marx jotted down the eleventh thesis and then, much later, tore philosophy from the privileged position it had once enjoyed. Although it might be the case that Marx did not intend this thesis to be anything more than a particular critique of Feuerbach and the way of doing philosophy that Feuerbach himself was attempting to critique, his claims about interpretation and transformation have taken on a life beyond what he might have intended. Moreover, if we read this thesis in light of the entire Marxist project from *Capital* onwards we have no choice but to interpret/demarcate it (which is the practice of philosophy) in the way I have suggested.

Whether or not we recognize this fact that philosophy has been transformed since the Marxist break matters little; if philosophy persists it must do so, either consciously or unconsciously, in the shadow of this transformation. The pretensions inherent to the world of philosophy were in fact changed by radical theory so that this world could stand revealed for what it had always been: the practice of interpretation. A philosophy consciously aware of this humble role, however, is the only philosophy capable of thinking of the larger world in a transformative manner; a philosophical practice that rejects this radical rupture belongs to the past, regardless of the "modern" ways in which some of its tendencies attempt to reject the emergence of Marxism.

Indeed, philosophical practice is meaningless without accepting the fact of that terrain which demands its reorientation. To deny the significance of the eleventh thesis is to cling to a philosophical corpse that was putrefying even before Marx drew a line between interpretation and transformation and thus simultaneously enabled the transformation of the former. There can be no philosophical practice that matters—that can demand clarification, force the possibility of annihilation, or even direct our attention towards transformation—if it denies the terrain from which social and historical truths are generated. After all, philosophy is a social practice, an historical activity.

Of course, philosophy continues to generate innumerable thinkers and practices that deny the significance of Marxism, sometimes violently so, and it would be somewhat wrong-headed to equally deny the value of such tendencies. By now we should be aware of the dogmatism evinced by those Marxists who, upon encountering a philosopher who disagrees with their political commitments, deny the totality of this philosopher's thought. Rather than advocating outright and dogmatic denial, then, we should gauge the worth of these philosophies and philosophers according to the distance between them and historical materialism...and the measuring of this distance is also the business of philosophy. Similarly, in the face of those scientific terrains that have significantly altered our understanding of reality, we have gauged the worth of past philosophical practices and, despite finding them wanting, have not simply relegated them to history's dust-heap. Indeed, those philosophers who lived before Darwin are not treated as worthless simply because they were incapable of grasping modern biology.

What we have, then, is a ruptural moment for philosophy. If historical materialism is a terrain that brings with its emergence and development the most radical demystification to *all* terrains and practices, then to practise philosophy without recognizing this demystification is to reject philosophy altogether. After all, the practice of philosophy is supposed to force clarity and, as discussed in previous chapters, demystification is the strongest forcing of clarity. And yet philosophy has been hampered by mystification since its inception, a reflection of a haunted world, and even became the bastion for mystification during the European Enlightenment when demystification was aimed at other aspects of thought. Hence we have the speculative philosophical systems of Kant and Hegel operating simultaneous to the development of Newtonian science, following the Copernican Revolution.[4] Newton himself shored up his superstition in philosophy, adopting the most mystic understandings in thought that were opposed to the very reality he was demystifying.

To practise philosophy in the shadow of the eleventh thesis, and to be unaware of this shadow, is to continue interpreting the world without realizing what it means to interpret a world that is demystified. In some cases this might mean a return to the speculative realm of grand ontologies; in other cases it might mean the most positivist practices of analytical philosophy. On the whole, however, a refusal to recognize the importance of this shadow is to fail to understand the necessity of changing the world. Rather, philosophy, ought to be placed in the service of transformation.

Spheres of practice

In order to wrap up this final chapter we can summarize the relationship of philosophy to transformation by looking at three overlapping spheres of practice: concrete, theoretical, and philosophical. Because these spheres overlap it is incorrect to assume that they possess a temporal order (i.e. first there is x, then there is y, and finally z), or that they are always completely distinct (I have already discussed the problem of assimilationism), but conceptually they should be treated as discreet zones of practice so as to clarify their meaning *and* understand that there is very good reason to assume, in the context of "transforming the world", that there is an order of conceptual priority. To make such a judgement is indeed a philosophical decision, as Laruelle would put it, but such a decision does not need to be seen as foundational: it only matters when we are talking according to the logic of the third sphere of practice, philosophy, which comes late.

The first and most fundamental sphere is *concrete practice*: social transformation is primarily achieved by movements that engage in social investigation and organize real people in a real-world state of affairs. The second sphere, which is initially generated by the first, is *theoretical-practice*: without a revolutionary movement, to temporarily reverse Lenin's formula, there can be no revolutionary theory; a unifying theory of struggle which might become a distinct theoretical terrain is conceptualized by the concrete analysis of a concrete situation that can only emerge from concrete practice but, in turn, brings coherence to this first sphere of practice—it even theorizes concepts such as "social investigation" and "concrete practice", turning spontaneous organizational practices into conceptual formations. The third sphere, the concern of this book, is *philosophical practice*: the practice of clarifying and interpreting the boundaries of the second sphere that, through this intervention, demarcates and forces meaning.

These distinct spheres are not limited to anti-capitalist struggle, though I find this problematic to be the most immediate and interesting. In the natural sciences, for example, we can think of the concrete practice of the laboratory where the messiness of scientific investigation is engaged with the tools that have developed through past concrete practices. The concrete scientific practice results in theorization, the moment where a coherent form is given to vague empirical engagement. And finally, scientific theories raise philosophical questions: they demand clarity, debate over the meaning of scientific theorization. Of course, the conceptual priority I have placed on these practices does not deny the dialectic between the first and second spheres. Due to the fact that scientific investigation does not take place outside of history, the concrete practice of the laboratory proceeds according to theoretical categories generated/established by previous moments of concrete practice...But the reason why concrete practice is primary is due to the fact that it might, at certain conjunctural moments, encounter a ruptural moment with pre-existing theory. Here is another moment where the sphere of philosophical practice becomes interesting: to clarify the ramifications, to struggle against "spontaneous philosophy", of a possible rupture while also grasping the meaning of its simultaneous unity.

We can also look to the realm of the arts to elucidate these spheres of practice. When artists are creating new movements with new styles they are involved in that moment of experimentation that is concrete practice. When such movements are given a particular form and are determined *as* movements this is the moment of theoretical-practice where the messiness of concrete practice is conceptualized. And finally, the boundaries of the conceptualized art movements are demarcated and interpreted by a philosophical practice: what does this group of artists, at this point in time, declaring x actually mean?

Since this book is primarily concerned with the philosophy of Marxism, however, I would prefer to focus on the way the spheres are related to the terrain of revolutionary theory. This terrain, as I have argued, is fundamental for our understanding of other terrains and in fact motivates a political decision regarding philosophy—that is, how philosophy is practised in regards to not only Marxism but also to other theoretical terrains.

Overall the dialectic between the spheres of concrete and theoretical-practice are fundamental: the former allows for the latter's emergence but the latter provides coherence for the former. While it is indeed the case that without a movement there can be no theory it is also the case that without a theory the movement cannot be coherently known as a movement. The feedback/circulation between these two spheres is what we can call *praxis*. But philosophical practice is more abstract since at first its practical sphere seems to exist outside of this dialectic as the comprehension of the dialectic itself: it is a second-order dialogue concerned with making sense of the meaning between the concrete and theoretical spheres so as to grasp the boundaries of a theoretical terrain—the denouement machine that attempts to force an understanding of the theoretical truth procedures (and these procedures' foundation of practice) towards a conclusion. "These struggles and practices, and the theoretical claims they produce," the philosopher declares, "should lead us into thinking x about this general terrain."

While it may indeed be the case that placing philosophical practice at the end of this sequence of practices might produce a teleological privileging of the practice of philosophy (where philosophy, though coming late, gets to declare the overall purpose of the spheres that form the dialectic of praxis) such a concern is also philosophical. We need to be clear: the dialectic of praxis will proceed with or without philosophy and the philosophical sphere of practice, which always comes too late, is only significant in that it attempts to demarcate the meaning of a truth procedure that will develop with or without philosophy. All of the conceptual terms that are wagered to explain such a truth procedure are indeed part of a particular philosophical decision; at the same time, though, this decision matters only for the realm of philosophy. We are mainly trying to illuminate, in philosophical terms, what the real movement to end the current state of affairs is doing with or without philosophy's intervention. Philosophical practice, which cannot help but declare the meaning of these other practices according to its own terms, will always come too late. Its decision, if and when it matters, will be determined by the contours of the theoretical terrain; as a denouement machine it will work to generate meaning based on the plot which it has been fed.

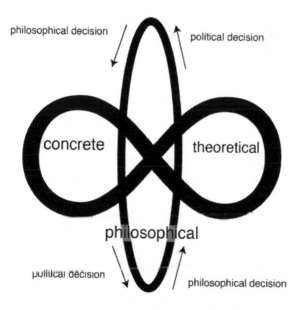

The theoretical terrain is the result of the circuit between the concrete and theoretical spheres of practice. Again, the circuit forming the topography of the terrain is what is called *praxis*. The dialectic between the concrete and the theoretical should be self-evident: a real-life movement, if it is to remain vital, generates a theoretical apprehension of its motion; theoretical-practice gives this movement its coherence and unity. Thus, while on the one hand it is correct to assert that without a revolutionary movement there can be no revolutionary theory, it is simultaneously correct to also state, as Lenin has, that without revolutionary theory there can be no revolutionary movement.

The sphere of philosophical practice, while being an intervention upon the concrete-theoretical circuit, is also produced by this dialectic. Although the sphere of philosophy is not part of the dialectical circuit of the other two spheres its practice is motivated by a political decision that is necessitated by this circuit (the need for clarity and demarcation) in a particular terrain and is in fact only possible because of the philosopher's experience and understanding of the circuit. The practice of philosophy becomes a philosophical decision in the Laruellian sense when it intervenes upon the terrain of the circuit. But this intervention is never uncompromised, as discussed in the third chapter, and the practice of philosophy is also altered at the moment of intervention, forcing another political decision that again motivates another philosophical decision, and the cycle of intervention continues in tandem with the circuit that it bisects.

The denouement machine chugs along. I am motivated to philosophically engage with a terrain to make sense of a given problematic; my understanding of the problematic is affected by this engagement and thus forces another intervention, based on this philosophical social intervention, which in turn results in another political decision, and the cycle continues. Meanwhile the theoretical terrain, which may also absorb the boundaries demarcated upon its topography by this philosophical intervention, continues its topographic development according to the circuit of praxis so that the cycle of philosophical intervention will eventually be forced to deal with new regions of thought.

Let us imagine that a philosopher is dealing with the problem of the revolutionary party as presented by Leninism which is the result of the praxis circuit, namely a revolutionary movement and a theory regarding this movement. The philosophical concern is how to make sense of a party that claims to organize the proletariat but comes "from outside". Depending on the philosopher's engagement with concrete and theoretical struggle, and depending on the way the circuit of praxis develops, there are different ways in which the cycle of philosophical praxis proceeds. If the philosopher is not committed to the Leninist circuit they will make a philosophical decision motivated by a political decision that has no patience with this terrain: they will treat this problematic as an outright contradiction and all engagement with this terrain will be to force this point. If the philosopher is committed to the Leninist circuit they will, upon trying to make sense of the apparent contradiction, be forced to think through its vicissitudes, be remotivated by other political decisions, and this remotivation will result in further philosophical interventions. At the same time, however, it might be the case that the circuit of praxis results in its own transformation where the topography is altered and thus the very theory of the party, and a concrete practice regarding the party, develops the theoretical terrain as a whole. Suddenly the philosopher interested in making sense of the meaning of the revolutionary party is forced to deal with new concepts (the mass-line, the party as a possible bastion for the bourgeoisie, an altered conception of proletariat and class struggle) as they pass again through the theoretical terrain. Political decisions are demanded at each and every moment of philosophical practice, especially if the philosopher is consciously engaged with the struggle that informs the circuit of praxis.[5]

And yet the above diagram's simplicity is deceptive. The practice of philosophy is not simply a sphere that cuts through a single circuit of practice, let alone just the one to which the philosopher is devoted. Philosophers intervene upon various theoretical terrains. The diagram is better conceived as a multiplicity of overlays and palimpsests.

To avoid the vagueness of abstraction, let's examine a concrete example where philosophical practice is applied to a series of theoretical terrains, cutting through each one to demarcate the terrain from which it itself originates. Anuradha Ghandy's brilliant essay "Philosophical Trends in the Feminist Movement" is a concise illustration of these interlinked spheres of practice although, keeping to the rubric established in this book so far, it might be more accurate to rename it "Theoretical Trends in the Feminist Movement". Motivated by a terrain of revolutionary communism, and particularly a fidelity to what would eventually be called *proletarian feminism*, Ghandy's essay is a philosophical intervention on various feminist sub-terrains—liberal feminism, radical feminism, socialist feminism, etc.—that are formed by circuits of concrete and theoretical-practice. As Arundhati Roy writes, Ghandy "takes us on a basic guided tour of a history of these movements, with quick thumb-nail analyses of various ideologies, ticking off their advantages and drawbacks like a teacher correcting an examination paper with a thick fluorescent marker".[6] In other words, the essay is an example of philosophical practice that is drawing a series of demarcations in the zones of praxis through which it cuts. The entire exercise is motivated by fidelity to the "Maoist perspective"[7] and thus intended to force the following perspective:

Not understanding women's oppression as linked to the wider exploitative socio-economic and political structure, to imperialism, [these particular variants of feminism] have sought solutions within the imperialist system itself. These solutions have at best benefited a section of middle class women but left the vast mass of oppressed and exploited women far from liberation. The struggle for women's liberation cannot be successful in isolation from the struggle to overthrow the imperialist system itself.[8]

Because Ghandy's essay is an example of philosophical practice she does not provide a theory that can answer the above critique, derived from the practice of multiple demarcations. Her essay can only force the reader to recognize the necessity of such a theory by unveiling the meaning of the theories she has investigated and interpreted. In doing so Ghandy draws the reader's attention to the theoretical terrain upon which she herself stands (the "Maoist perspective"), simultaneously implying that it has the tools with which to answer her concerns but that it has not yet used these tools to generate this theoretical development. Since Ghandy wrote this essay the demand forced by her philosophical practice has indeed influenced organizers and organic intellectuals to think and develop the concept of proletarian feminism. In this sense, while the current trend of theorizing and debating the concept of proletarian feminism was necessitated by Ghandy's philosophical decision(s), it is not the product of an a priori philosophical decision as Laruelle would have us believe; the philosophical decisions made upon various circuits of praxis were in fact motivated by the political decision of her militant fidelity to her own theoretical terrain *and* other political decisions pulled out of multiple interventions upon each zone of feminist theory.

Hence philosophical practice is always invested in the circuits of praxis. If it has anything to contribute to these circuits it is only to clarify for those engaged in concrete and theoretical struggle the possible terms of the concrete-theoretical dialectic. That is, to clarify the spheres that can determine real-world transformation. We philosophers leap out of this circuit only to imagine that we are like Sriduangkaew's character Ziyi: comets descending to decide the meaning of existence. But like Ziyi and the denouement machine of this speculative story, we are in fact compromised by the terrain, forced to make decisions based on our changing understanding of this terrain, and are thus forced back into the messy world of concrete theoretical-practice. In this story, after all, there is a point where Ziyi is compromised by the terrain: despite assuming she exists outside of the terrain upon which she is intervening, a representative of this terrain *bribes* her with proof that she is not perfectly autonomous.[9] The philosopher is never autonomous; the philosopher is always invested; the denouement machine that forces meaning is just as much a product of the theoretical terrain as it is the thing which is capable of drawing harsh lines of meaning. And without this terrain, and the transformation that is a necessary part of this terrain, the philosophical practice of interpretation would not exist.

Therefore, to claim that philosophers have only interpreted the world (but the point is to change it) should, according to this exhortation of practice, lead us out of the realm of philosophical decision and into the realm of *political* decision. Despite the fact that it decides philosophically on the meaning of a particular conceptual order, philosophy is a second-order intervention. Moreover the content of the philosophical decision—the ideological line, the philosopher's commitment/fidelity—is determined by this prior political decision forced by the philosopher's relation to a given theoretical terrain, even the one upon which they intervene.

Philosophy comes too late but its meaning is located in this lateness.

Notes
1.   Here it must be noted again that Popper's project was also

driven by an inability to reflect on his own ideological commitments. His attempt to provide foundational meaning to the sciences was connected to his anti-communism, determined by his desire to exclude historical materialism from his declaration of meaning.

2. This situation is not merely hypothetical. The late *Fuse* magazine's editorial board made the decision in 2014 to prematurely terminate the magazine (a periodical that possessed a history of anti-systemic radicalism but relied on the public-funding system) based on the assumption that austerity would make arts funding a thing of the past. I discussed this situation in a little more detail, and the way in which it represented a collaboration with austerity ideology, in *Austerity Apparatus* (Montreal: Kersplebedeb, 2017).

3. Hegel, *Elements of the Philosophy of Right*, 23.

4. As noted in the first chapter, Quentin Meillassoux and Bertrand Russell have suggested that Kant was in fact enacting a Ptolemaic counter-revolution.

5. An example of the cycle of philosophical practice regarding the problematic of the revolutionary party can be found in the third chapter of *Continuity and Rupture* (93-135). In this context I engaged and reengaged with the apparent contradiction of a proletarian party that comes from "the outside", according to the limits of Marxism-Leninism, while also noting how the emergence of Maoism altered this philosophical engagement by renewing the theoretical terrain.

6. Roy, xv.

7. Ghandy, 190.

8. Ibid., 199.

9. This moment comes in Šriduangkaew's story when the character Liatrice, the individual who in fact turned on the denouement machine, recruits Ziyi by threatening her

autonomy: "I've solved the puzzle of your immortality. Many of your orbits ago, in a city whose name you've erased and whose people you've exterminated, you were imprisoned for a turn of the sun. During that time you could be hurt; the strength of your body failed before bullets and disassembly fields. Eventually you could be cut by something as primitive as a knife. The myth of the comet must be held up on your end, or else you wither and become as mortal as any of us."

Epilogue

the political decision

The engine itself lies inert, frozen into its final shape. [...] It may prove a novelty, or more, with much to unlock and repurpose.
Benjamin Sriduangkaew, Comet's Call

In this treatise I have described the meaning of philosophy in the shadow of Marx's eleventh thesis, philosophy as a radical practice. Particularly, I have attempted to excavate what it means to practise a philosophy of Marxism and why this practice is the only way in which philosophy can proceed as an interpretive activity capable of forcing clarity and demystification as well as demanding transformation. The metaphor of cartography and the analogy of a terrain, not to be misunderstood as an ontological system, has been employed so as to make the meaning of philosophical practice clear.

I realize some readers will be disappointed with how I have conceptualized philosophy. When I wrote *Continuity and Rupture*, for example, some readers expected a formulation of "Maoist philosophy" rather than a philosophical interrogation of the meaning of Maoism. Similarly, I suspect that this book will fail to satisfy readers looking for a precise formulation of "Marxist philosophy" rather than a discussion of how philosophy can and should be understood in light of the emergence of Marxism. Unfortunately, as should be clear by now, I do not believe that there is a single formulation for a "Marxist philosophy"; instead there are numerous Marxist philosophies. As a historical materialist, then, I have laboured under the impression that it is better to try and define what philosophy means, specifically from the Marxist standpoint, rather than provide a textbook formula. I maintain that it is better to understand the long

197

practice of philosophy as Marxists, and the importance of making philosophical interventions, than what is proper and improper Marxist philosophy. Perhaps such a complaint, though, results from what I have not directly addressed, except as a point to make sense of the general meaning of a philosophy of Marxism: *the practice of the practice of philosophy*. That is, according to what logical method should our philosophical interventions be based? As noted at various moments in the previous pages, in order to explain philosophical meaning, some explanation of method, this question is often answered with the formula *dialectical materialism*.

In the first chapter I briefly discussed how a crude application of dialectical materialism, based on a formulaic conceptualization of the methodology inherited from the past, does not satisfy the demands of philosophical practice. Rather, what often results from such a doctrinaire practice is not necessarily the materialist method that the militants of "diamat" would hope but, instead, another theology where its "laws" attempt to provide the same speculative architecture as the preceding grand ontological systems. Aside from a few examples as to why this result was the case, along with some general comments, it would have been tangential to examine the problematic of methodology itself without first excavating the general meaning of philosophy (that is, the basis upon which I could even call the doctrinaire utilization of "diamat" pseudo-philosophical), as this treatise has hopefully succeeded in doing.

One solution to the lack of clarity surrounding dialectical materialism, proposed by Marxists who are either philosophers or interested in philosophy, is to return to Hegel. That is, recognizing that there is indeed an impoverished understanding of dialectical logic amongst Marxists a popular panacea is to declare that a thorough understanding of Hegel is necessary for Marxists, especially those in cadre organizations. After all, Lenin and Mao read Hegel and if we grant that these great revolutionaries were also brilliant dialecticians then we should follow their example. My position on this matter, as should be clear from the preceding chapters, is that the Marxist rupture in thought is such that we would completely misunderstand its theoretical terrain by subordinating it to a philosophical decision of the Laruellian type. Moreover, to subordinate our expertise in revolutionary science to the requirement of understanding the speculative philosophy of Hegel is an example of what I called, in the fifth chapter, *betrayal*.

All of the invectives to "return to Hegel" (made by Marxists on behalf of Marxism) fall apart once we recognize the philosophical injunction captured by the eleventh thesis. If Marx and Engels initiated a science that was intended to put philosophy in its place, to force it to tail materialist theory, then it makes no sense to demand a reinvestigation of Hegel or any other pre-Marxist philosopher in order to comprehend this theoretical sequence. The sequence is comprehensible in and of itself and does not require philosophical foundations; the demand for philosophical foundations is in fact anti-materialist, a holdover from a time where philosophers imagined that they determined the ground of reality. But if Marxism declared itself as the science of the proletariat then recourse to bourgeois philosophy is antithetical to this science: such a recourse demands that the working class become bourgeois philosophers rather than breaking from this practice altogether. *Capital* makes sense with or without Hegel; in fact, based on my own experience, I would argue that those who try to understand this text according to Hegel have a harder time appreciating its critique than a class conscious member of the working class who has never read a page of Hegel or any other canonical philosopher.

To demand that a proper understanding of Marx requires an understanding of Hegel becomes immediately absurd once we grasp the meaning of this invective. If the "truth" of Marxism can be located in one of its important influences (and, yes, we must admit that Hegel *was* such an influence) then we are presented with a hermeneutics that demands infinite regress. That is, if it is the case that Marx cannot be properly understood without Hegel because Hegel was an influence then, by the same token, we must conclude that Hegel cannot be properly understood without Kant. This is not empty theorizing but, in point of fact, the logical conclusion of the argument that an understanding of Marx demands an understanding of Hegel: once we appeal to one precedent as significant then, by the same token, we must recognize prior precedents. If Marx is not entirely comprehensible without studying Hegel then, according to the same logic, Hegel cannot be understood without studying Kant. This is not a leap in logic because, as anyone who has studied philosophy knows, Hegel's entire system largely exists in response to Kant. Just as Kant, accordingly, exists in reference to Hume and others. And so we keep pushing our understanding backwards until we discover the pre-Socratics. Unless we were to consider Hegel a rupture from all of philosophy to date, *but this is precisely what I have argued in regards to Marx.* That is, Marxism represents the theoretical rupture that severs itself from the chain of philosophical mystification for very clear, materialist reasons. Hegel does not represent this rupture and to claim otherwise would be completely arbitrary: once you deny the materialist rupture of Marxism and demand the foundation of Hegel then you must accept infinite regress because Hegel was part of the same philosophical project and Marxism, unlike Hegelianism, produces an entirely new understanding of philosophy. To presume otherwise is to reject Marxism *by definition*.

Hegel's system is one culmination (and for some *the* culmination) of philosophy-qua-philosophy, a complex ontological system—a "first philosophy" declaring itself the deep science of existence itself. While it is indeed the case that Marx was influenced by Hegel's systematization of dialectical logic, his aim was not to produce another first philosophy that sought to provide metaphysical foundations for all of science and logic but, instead, to initiate a materialist rupture from philosophy. The Marxist "science of history" is thus not Hegel's "science of logic" but in fact a materialist conception of history and society, historical materialism: a scientific theory intended to demystify its object of study rather than remystify it according to theological principles. In this sense the entire meaning of philosophy is altered. From the shadow of the eleventh thesis philosophy no longer appears as "the beginning of everything" or "the *absolute ground*"[1] but a practice that comes after theory, particularly scientific theory, in order to clarify and force—or alternately, obscure and occult—truth procedures. Philosophy is thus revealed as a machine for denouement rather than initiation. And whenever philosophical practice is presented as initiation, as first philosophy, what is really happening is that a denouement (the finale or climax of a chain of events) is being presented as origin. Such a confusion, which again we can compare to Laruelle's conception of "the philosophical decision" (keeping in mind our previous qualifications), often results in obfuscation and occultation.

The truth is that the practice of philosophy is a secondary requirement for the theoretical terrain initiated by Marx and Engels. To be a practitioner of their scientific theory does not require a sophisticated understanding of the history of philosophy since philosophy is no longer foundational. We would hope that philosophers working within the theoretical terrain of historical materialism would study the history of their discipline, but historical materialism does not belong to philosophers: it belongs to the proletariat; its prime theoreticians are proletarian scientists, revolutionary theorists.

Moreover, those Marxist philosophers who have sought to re establish the primacy of Hegel have often been thinkers largely opposed to revolutionary practice: Adorno and Horkheimer, Zizek, etc. Attempts to rephilosophize Marxism have always led to its academicization and reification. This entire treatise, it must be noted, began by rejecting this inverted version of the eleventh thesis. Historical materialism is wagered as the "real movement which abolishes the present state of things" rather than another school of philosophical contemplation: change rather than interpretation.

Even still, and despite my thoughts on a proposed return to Hegel, unanswered questions regarding the meaning of dialectical materialism—indeed, the very meaning of dialectical logic—do haunt this book. At the very least, they persisted by operating beneath the surface of this intervention, emerging briefly when they could not be contained, and it is necessary to address them in more detail. Indeed, the way in which I have engaged with the meaning of philosophy in general was guided by that methodological approach that sometimes goes by the name dialectical materialism—the "scaffolding", to recall Marx's letter to Engels regarding his abandonment of the *Grundrisse* in favour of *Capital*. Although it is clear that we should neither seek bastion in old formulae of dialectical materialism nor demand a return to Hegel (though investigating and learning from both is not discouraged let alone forbidden), questions surrounding the meaning and significance of dialectical materialism necessarily persist.

To attempt to answer these questions here, at the conclusion of this reflection on philosophy and the theoretical terrain, would be a mistake. On the one hand, it would feel tacked on to a discussion that concluded in the chapter above. On the other hand, such a tacking-on of the problematic of dialectical materialism would do damage to the object of thought, reducing it to another set of simple formulations. After all, if we are to examine the questions lurking behind the philosophical methodology of dialectical materialism we cannot help but be met with a history of dogmatic applications, innumerable "beginners books" intended to explain dialectics to the lay person, the ghost of

Hegel, the connection or contraposition between dialectical and formal logic that should not be dismissed, and why dialectical logic even matters in the concrete world of practice.[2]

But even if all accepted that dialectical materialism is the only methodological approach that deserves to be called "Marxist philosophy", we are still left with the quandary raised by this book: philosophy, no matter what logical methodology is employed, is about interpreting the world. No matter how insightful your dialectics are, no matter how precise your understanding of contradiction, they remain interpretive interventions designed to force denouement. Such interventions are important, and I have not argued otherwise, but we need to understand them for what they are rather than assign them a grandiose destiny. So if the intervention of philosophy upon the theoretical terrain is important but not as meaningful—in the sense that the former can only attempt to clarify/force meaning whereas the latter is the bedrock of meaning itself—then what is the meaning of its importance? Once again we return to the questions that initiated this project, the ancestral lineages our denouement machine has pursued: the meaning of that which clarifies meaning, the philosophy of philosophy.

The weaponization of philosophy

Years ago, when I first began this project, I was mainly interested in explaining my labour as a Marxist who is also a philosopher because I felt that the philosophical practice of Marxists was generally unclear, both to readers of this philosophy and philosophers themselves. What made my engagements with political economy, for example, the engagements of a philosopher rather than a political economist—what was the meaning of philosophical intervention? Since that time I have written and published four other books (for the last of which I was a co-author) that have been driven by the sensibility I've done my best to explain in the preceding pages. During this period of publication, I edited, expanded and rewrote the manuscript that is about to conclude. To practise philosophical intervention is to change and alter my understanding of the practice; doubtless, in a few more years following other publications, I could have expanded and transformed this manuscript further.

In order to pursue this project I was forced to go back to the work of Althusser, a thinker I had at one time written off, only to discover that the contours of my argument were already drafted in his own attempt to make sense of philosophy from a Marxist position. In fact, I ended up making significant edits on what I had hoped was a completed draft when his *Philosophy for Non-Philosophers* was finally published. Simultaneous to this rediscovery of Althusser was an encounter with a decidedly anti-intellectual strain of Marxism (masquerading as populist so as to hide its own elitist assumption of the "dumb masses") that treated philosophy as either useless or a priori inaccessible. Often these two encounters intersected: Sean Ledwith's review of *Philosophy for Non-Philosophers* dismisses Althusser for being inaccessible and claims instead that people should read the likes of Tony Cliff—indicating a complete dismissal of philosophical practice since Cliff was not a philosopher.[3] This Ledwith example demonstrates that even amongst the intellectual gatekeepers of Marxist thought there is very little understanding about what philosophy is as an historical practice. It is thus telling that one of the only books that attempted to provide a thorough historical materialist account of philosophy, from its emergence to its persistence in the bourgeois order, was dismissed and misrepresented.

The worry, then, is that any explanation of my own project will be doomed to the classification of "inaccessible" from the outset. After all, since its emergence philosophy has accumulated so much clutter that all attempts to demystify its history are forced to deal with this clutter and do their best to render accessible what has become inaccessible. Hence the problem my own practice is stuck with is two-fold: i) how to make certain that my interventions serve the broader class struggle; ii) how to explain the meaning of such interventions in a manner that does not get lost in the fog of philosophical obscurantism. And in both cases intellectuals who are philosophical laypersons, though often very adept in their own areas of expertise (whether these be history, political economy, sociology, etc.), will intervene to declare whether or not I am doing philosophy without having an idea of what philosophy is. The deeper question, then, is whether practising philosophy and attempting to explain the meaning of this practice even matters.

I think that it does matter and, despite the problems we necessarily encounter, also believe that providing an anatomy of this practice is useful. Let me explain...

First of all, the ruling ideas of the ruling class are defended by multiple philosophers, many of whom are under the impression that they are simply being reasonable, that they labour outside of class struggle. Philosophy is a weapon for the bourgeoisie; its historical interventions upon the terrain of bourgeois ideology have provided arguments and justifications for the bourgeois order. We don't have to work very hard to prove that this is the case: look at utilitarian thought, from Bentham and Austin's legal positivism to Mill's harm principle, and we cannot help but see the basis of all the liberal arguments that justify the current order even to the point of defending fascism. Or look at Popper's influential declaration of the meaning of science that was primarily intended to exclude historical materialism from rational thought. If we are ever to succeed in building a hegemony that dislodges the bourgeois order "the proletariat too needs a philosophy of its own that *adjusts* the ensemble of its ideological arms for class combat".[4]

Secondly, a refusal to comprehend and thus foster philosophical practice has resulted in a kind of magical thinking on the part of large swathes of the anti-capitalist left. In believing they already know the meaning of philosophy, that they do not have to foster a philosophical practice, they will allow theory to persist without ideological struggle beyond reifying lazy interventions. On the one hand there are the movementists who refuse to think through the limits of an aimless theoretical-practice, who might not even wish to think about the meaning of theoretical terrains. On the other hand there are the Marxist-Leninist dogmatists who, despite the failure of the Soviet Union, repeat the "philosophical" dogmas about the laws of dialectical materialism and assume that philosophy is a ready-made wish fulfilment algorithm. Both poles are unified in their disdain for the possibility of a proletarian philosophy, even if and when they declare their love of philosophy, because neither is interested in producing a practice of class struggle upon the terrain of theory—they see their perspectives as already legitimated, they advance disarmed.

Philosophy is indeed a weapon, the clarity and forcing of meaning inherent to its practice is essential to ideological warfare, and this book was an attempt to demonstrate why this is the case. Philosophy is that vast and terrible denouement machine from Sriduangkaew's story, a frightening apparatus that traces and targets lines of flight: it is ineffable to those who refuse to recognize its significance, its meaning is clear to the militant who takes a position, it is bound to the strictures of the terrain upon which it is determined to make its decision, but it can be nothing more than a weapon. A weapon that forces meaning, draws together the various strands of the terrain upon which it operates, declares a position.

Clarity-through-struggle

Interpreting the world, though important to provide clarity, is not enough. The point, as Marx asserted, is transformation. We continue to interpret the world even though we are supposed to be concerned with this world's transformation. At the very least, for those of us whose philosophical interventions are focused on the Marxist terrain, the interpretative gesture should be focused so as to draw attention to the meaning of Marxism: while philosophy cannot change the world, it should be able to point out the fact that Marxism *should* be aimed at changing the world and interrogate what Marxisms are best equipped to fulfil this demand.

Part of the clarifying, demystifying and demarcating role that a principled and critical philosophical practice will play in pursuing the above task will be in the merciless criticism of dogmatism. While it is indeed the case that revolutionary movements producing the theory necessary to develop the terrain will produce their own safe-guards against dogmatism, the practice of philosophy is a weapon in this regard. We know that dogmatism can creep into any movement where philosophical struggle upon the terrain of theory is disallowed. Unfortunately there often emerges a tendency to dismiss philosophical practice, to relegate the interpretative gesture of philosophy to oblivion, and to proceed according to anti-intellectual formalism. We can see evidence of this anti-intellectualism in various Marxist tendencies where an uncritical quote mining of key texts functions as substitution for critical investigation. Rigorous theoretical study is discouraged (sometimes branded "academic", the preferred anti-intellectual insult for any form of study), historical investigation is distorted, and work that challenges formulaic and simple narratives is misrepresented and/or dismissed. The weapon of philosophy, which advocates wholesale theoretical investigation and intervention, is the best solution to this problem, but only if it is also bound to a political project and is diffused amongst every militant of this project so it is not simply the practice of the specialist. Politics is indeed, as Sylvain Lazarus has claimed, "the order of thought",[5] and yet at the same time the ordering of thought and the approach to thinking is also a political decision.

Hence, the philosophy of Marxism is not conditioned by what Laruelle called the "philosophical decision"; it is determined by the *political decision*. (Indeed, as Badiou argues, all philosophies are conditioned by "a real politics".) In the beginning it is conditioned by the decision to become involved in a political project or retreat into reflection. As Morera writes in reference to Gramsci:

> The aim of philosophical reflection, though often expressed in academic language is, like Gramsci's, a political one in the broadest sense. That is, it is a process of creating a critical, coherent view of the world rooted in the common sense of a people without being a mere reproduction of all its beliefs.[6]

Moreover, since the political reality of class struggle ought to lead the philosopher of Marxism to be a Marxist in the world as a whole rather than the rarified world of reflection, which was Marx's exhortation in his eleventh thesis, then the political decision opens up other dilemmas that require similar prior decisions. The fact that philosophy will necessarily tail the truth procedures of theory, and thus must recognize its vocation to clarify and demarcate the theoretical terrain, demands a constant unfolding of the political decision: on what project do we stake our philosophical labour, in what movement do we practise philosophy while also practising its politics? Here the decision of philosophy is not a priori but is in fact recursive in that it becomes a reflection of the political decision as it clarifies and justifies a chosen theoretical terrain.

Of course, the philosophy of Marxism has something useful to say about how and why we should choose one political decision over another, and a skilled philosopher only comes to accept a particular political trajectory because they have done the hard work of clarifying and demarcating the already existing theoretical terrain. At the same time, however, the only reason the philosopher imagines they have the right to reserve their opinion about one Marxist trajectory over another is because they have initially declared fidelity to the political decision Marx already made: change over interpretation, practice over reflection—these are not the decisions of philosophy but the decisions of concrete and visceral politics. Any attempt to philosophically decide what this political decision means will necessarily, if we are honest, catapult us into the realm of praxis.

The philosopher of Marxism becomes a Marxist philosopher when they grasp the initial political decision of change and practice, dedicate themselves to a militant project, serve this project to the best of their abilities, and have come to this dedication and practice because of their fidelity to the primary political decision of class struggle. After such a decision has been made, the practice of philosophy will be conditioned by the order of the politics it has accepted. The philosopher of Marxism will finally become the Marxist philosopher when they become a militant invested in an emancipatory project and make the conscious decision to ground their training in service to this project. Does this make the Marxist philosopher a propagandist for a political project? Yes, but we cannot escape generating propaganda if we understand propaganda to be the manifestation of an ideological line: the philosopher who is not a militant, who imagines that they are outside of the class struggle, will end up generating propaganda for the current state of affairs while imagining that they are free from the taint of political commitment. It should not be surprising, then, that every political philosopher who imagines they are outside of class struggle does little more than replicate liberal ideology.

In this sense, to interpret the world is to support a praxis of change by, through the very act of drawing demarcating lines and forcing a choice, arguing for the veracity of one approach over another—to force a choice regarding the political decision. Not that this gesture should confuse itself with the practice of making change: good arguments solve nothing, a revolutionary movement producing theory as it draws people into its orbit is worth more than a thousand philosophical arguments. Again: philosophy tails theory, arriving upon a pre-existing terrain to perform the task—awkwardly or with sophistication, sloppily or rigorously—of demarcation.

To bring us back to the analogy with which I began this project, the philosopher is akin to Sriduangkaew's character Hu Ziyi who falls from the sky to force meaning alongside the operations of a machine demarcating a pre-existing terrain. Philosophy as a denouement machine, an operation that draws the narrative strands of a theoretical terrain together, a weapon wielded against the ancestral lines of enemy terrains; the philosopher as the agent who engages with this operation/weapon in the interest of clarity-through-struggle. And like Ziyi, the philosopher is also and always implicated in their decision. Therefore, although it is vital to at least *begin* by correctly interpreting the world, the realm of interpretation will always lag behind the theoretical terrain that itself emerges from the realm of practice. Here is where philosophy is abandoned, that rupture signified by Marx's eleventh thesis, and where change begins.

Notes

1. Hegel, *Logic*, 67
2. I tried to write such a book once and, after a single failed submission, decided that I was disinterested in pursuing this project. A completed draft of that attempt that I do not feel is wholly satisfactory, *Torsion and Tension*, is available on my blog.
3. http://marxandphilosophy.org.uk/reviewofbooks/reviews/2017/2756
4. Althusser, *Philosophy for Non-Philosophers*, 179.
5. Lazarus, 1.
6. Morera, *Gramsci, Materialism, and Philosophy*, 22-23.

Works Cited

Adorno, Theodor W. *Negative Dialectics*. New York: Continuum, 2000.

Althusser, Louis. *For Marx*. London: Verso, 1997.

Althusser, Louis. *On the Reproduction of Capitalism*. London: Verso, 2014.

Althusser, Louis. *Philosophy and the Spontaneous Philosophy of the Scientists*. London: Verso, 2011.

Althusser, Louis. *Philosophy for Non-Philosophers*. London: Bloomsbury, 2017.

Amin, Samir. *Eurocentrism (2nd Edition)*. New York: Monthly Review Press, 2009.

Amin, Samir. *Spectres of Capitalism: a critique of current intellectual fashion*. New York: Monthly Review Press, 1998.

Badiou, Alain. *Being and Event*. London: Continuum, 2005.

Badiou, Alain. *Ethics: an essay on the understanding of evil*. London: Verso, 2012.

Badiou, Alain. *Logics of Worlds*. London: Bloomsbury, 2013.

Badiou, Alain. *Metapolitics*. London: Verso, 2006.

Badiou, Alain. *Polemics*. London: Verso, 2006.

Badiou, Alain. *Theory of the Subject*. London: Bloomsbury, 2012.

Balibar, Etienne. *The Philosophy of Marx*. London: Verso, 2014.

Baudrillard, Jean. *Simulacra and Simulation*. Michigan: University of Michigan Press, 2000.

Benjamin, Walter. *Illuminations*. New York: Schocken Books, 1968.

Brassier, Ray. *Nihil Unbound: Enlightenment and Extinction*. London: Palgrave-Macmillan, 2010.

Code, Lorraine. *Rhetorical Spaces: Essays on Gendered Locations*. London: Routledge, 1995.

Delany, Samuel R. *Stars In My Pocket Like Grains of Sand*. New York: Bantam Books, 1985.

Engels, Friedrich. *Anti-Duhring and Dialectics of Nature*. New York: International Publishers, 1987.

Engels, Friedrich. *Ludwig Feuerbach and the End of Classical German Philosophy*. Peking: Foreign Languages Press, 1976.

Fanon, Frantz. *The Wretched of the Earth*. New York: Grove Press, 1963.

Feuerbach, Ludwig. *The Fiery Brook: Selected Writings*. London: Verso, 2012.

Ghandy, Anuradha. *Scripting the Change: the selected writings of Anuradha Ghandy*. Delhi: Daanish Books, 2011.

Hallward, Peter and Knox Peden (Eds). *Concept and Form: Key Texts From the Cahiers pour l'Analyse (Volume One)*. London: Verso, 2012.

Hatoum, Mona. *Mona Hatoum: The Entire World As A Foreign Land*. London: Tate Gallery Publishing, 2000.

Hegel, G.W.F. *Elements of the Philosophy of Right*. Cambridge: Cambridge University Press, 1991.

Hegel, G.W.F. *Science of Logic*. Amherst: Humanity Books, 1969.

Horkheimer, Max and Theodor W. Adorno. *Dialectic of Enlightenment*. New York: Continuum, 2001.

Laruelle, François. *Dictionary of Non-Philosophy*. Minneapolis: Univocal Publishing, 2013.

Laruelle, François. *Introduction to Non-Marxism*. Minneapolis: Univocal Publishing, 2015.

Laruelle, François. *Philosophy and Non-Philosophy*. Minneapolis: Univocal Publishing, 2013.

Laruelle, François. *Principles of Non-Philosophy*. London: Bloomsbury, 2013.

Lazarus, Sylvain. *Anthropology of the Name*. London: Seagull Books, 2015.

Lee, Butch and Red Rover. *Night-Vision: illuminating class & war in the neo-colonial terrain*. New York: Vagabond Press, 1993.

Marx, Karl. *The 18th Brumaire of Louis Bonaparte*. New York: International Publishers, 1969.

Marx, Karl. *Grundrisse*. London: Penguin Books, 1993.

Marx, Karl and Friedrich Engels. *The German Ideology*. Amherst: Prometheus Books, 1998.

Meillassoux, Quentin. *After Finitude: an essay on the necessity of contingency*. London: Bloomsbury, 2014.

Morera, Esteve. *Gramsci's Historicism: a realist interpretation*. London: Routledge, 2011.

Morera, Esteve. *Gramsci, Materialism, and Philosophy*. London: Routledge, 2014.

Moufawad-Paul, J. *The Communist Necessity*. Montreal: Kersplebedeb, 2014.

Moufawad-Paul, J. *Continuity and Rupture: Philosophy in the Maoist Terrain*. Winchester: Zero Books, 2016.

Rancière, Jacques. *Proletarian Nights: The Workers' Dream in Nineteenth-Century France*. London: Verso, 2012.

Rancière, Jacques. *Staging the People: the Proletarian and his Double*. London: Verso, 2011.

Roy, Arundhati. "...But Anuradha was different." In Ghandy, Anuradha: *Scripting the Change* (Delhi: Daanish Books, 2011), xi-xv.

Shaw, Devin Zane. *Egalitarian Moments: from Descartes to Rancière*. London: Bloomsbury, 2016.

Schmidt, Alfred. *The Concept of Nature in Marx*. London: Verso, 2014.

Wittgenstein, Ludwig. *Tractatus Logico-Philosophicus*. London: Routledge, 2002.

Wright, Erik Olin. *Classes*. London: Verso, 1997.

Yami, Hisila. *People's War and Women's Liberation in Nepal*. Kathmandu: Janadhwani Publications, 2007.

Acknowledgements

There are a lot of people to thank, many who might not make it onto this list because of a memory failure on my part and to whom I apologize in advance. As I have maintained in the acknowledgement sections of my previous books, no act of knowledge production exists in a void; multiple voices, some of which are already multiple, are always present. The author is not an independent agent, a self-created maverick. In the context of this polyphony, though, there are always some voices that are more noticeable, that I can clearly recognize in the creative cacophony, that deserve acknowledgement. Since this is a book about philosophy then it is only appropriate I begin by recognizing my teachers and fellow travellers in that discipline.

First off, I would like to thank Jeff Noonan, the philosopher who served as my thesis supervisor when I was pursuing my MA. While it is the case that we have political disagreements, he was my first encounter with the practice of the philosophy of Marxism. I have him to thank for waking me from my anarchist "dogmatic slumber" and teaching me the strength of historical materialism. Whatever our differences now, Jeff's critical work on liberalism and post-modernism and his development of a theory of a material life-ground for ethics remain precious resources.

Secondly, I must thank Esteve Morera, my doctorate supervisor, who I would eventually discover, years after my PhD defence, had influenced me in more ways than I originally assumed. It was only when I finished his important book on Gramsci, *Gramsci's Historicism* (a must read for anyone who is interested in studying Gramsci), a couple years back that I realized how much of my philosophical approach was conditioned by his subtle and humble instruction. My obsession over precision regarding the distinction between name and concept, which finds its way into all my work, can be located in Esteve's philosophical practice (even if he's not its originator); my desire for clarity and a systemic approach to what at first appears fragmentary, something I have still not perfected, is inherited from his methodological concerns. Esteve might be the fundamental reason I wrote this book on the philosophy of Marxism since, when I first set out to start an earlier and much impoverished draft, I was motivated by comments he had made, long ago, on my dissertation proposal: how is this philosophy, what about your approach makes this a philosophical project? These were not questions designed to protect philosophy as a discipline from the interdisciplinary practice that is often encouraged in graduate studies but, rather, an encouragement to think deeper into the basis of my academic training vis-a-vis Marxism. Indeed, when he made these criticisms in the second year of my PhD after I turned in the draft of my thesis proposal he contextualized them according to the question of this book: in light of multiple interpretations of "Marxist philosophy" (and he listed several of these interpretations, the categories listed in my first chapter, by Marxists x, y, z) how did I conceive of my philosophical project in the Marxist terrain? Since I didn't really answer this question in my dissertation, though I did provide an introductory qualification about my philosophical approach to my chosen object of critique (i.e. ongoing settler-colonialism and what theoretical approach to this problematic was necessitated by this objective fact) that satisfied him enough to accept my dissertation project, this book might be the proper answer to that question so many years later.

Thirdly, the second reader of my doctoral dissertation also deserves significant recognition, particularly since some of her work found its way into this book. Lorraine Code, feminist epistemologist and clear-headed philosopher extraordinaire, influenced and encouraged me throughout my PhD education. I'm honoured by the fact that she agreed to be my second reader right when she was retiring; before that decision I had worked for her as a Teaching Assistant for multiple years in her second year Existentialism course. Although I never had the privilege of taking one of her graduate courses (they were either offered at times that conflicted with my job or were offered when I was no longer taking courses), all of the personal, political, and philosophical discussions with her in the years I worked as her TA and after were extremely precious. Her lovingly caustic encouragement cut through a lot of the bullshit of philosophy training and taught me what it should mean to think philosophy as a radical practice. I have fond memories of the time, during the second year I worked for her, when Lorraine met with me and said "you study Fanon, so let's put some Fanon on the Existentialist syllabus". Or when she rigorously combed through one of my dissertation chapters and then summarized everything I was saying by quoting a Brecht poem. Or when she met with me the morning of my defence, hugged me, and told me not to worry because my dissertation was "masterful". Or when, after I published my first book, she pointed out it had no dedication to anyone, that maybe it should be dedicated to my wife and daughter, and joked "you man, you". Despite not proclaiming fidelity to a Marxist project, her work on epistemology (as I have argued in this book) is guided by the principles of the kind of philosophy of Marxism I defend: whose knowledge and for whom.

Fourthly, my anarchist (or maybe "post-anarchist") double Gabriel Kuhn again deserves acknowledgement. Although we have never met in person (at least at the moment I am writing this acknowledgement) the long-term email exchange between us that was initiated by his critical review of my first book remains a source of intellectual inspiration. In this context, some of the questions he asked about my definition of philosophy after reading a draft of *Continuity and Rupture* (that he wrote an endorsement for) guided the manner in which I returned to an earlier draft of this book. I'm looking forward to the day when we finally meet in person and can discuss all of these problematics over a coffee at the margins of *Moominland*.

Fifthly, my colleague and friend Jon Short deserves recognition. Despite his higher tolerance for Derrida, his grasp and articulation of many of the thinkers I have used in this book has been both insightful and influential. He also shared my suspicion, despite being an Agamben scholar, of the academic left's flirtation with Schmitt before others wised up to this problem. The first time I seriously read Badiou was in a *Being and Event* reading group Jon and some other friends initiated about a decade ago; many of our discussions since then have been guided by conversations that began in that group. Jon: I bet you're laughing at the fact that I put Laruelle to use after listening to me complain about him for years.

Next, I want to thank the multiple union comrades with whom I have walked the picket lines in 2008-2009, 2015, and 2018. As I prepared this manuscript for submission the 2018 strike was reaching its denouement, after my unit shamefully settled (its bargaining team members collaborating with the employer and organizing anti-union radicals to support this collaboration), leaving Teaching Assistants and Graduate Assistants to walk the lines. The philosophy department was always underrepresented in this trilogy of strikes, with many of our colleagues falling into the trap of bourgeois philosophy (some of whom were openly reactionary), and others drifting through the strike because they somehow felt it was less real than their studies. The philosophy of academia is not the philosophy of the proletariat, and those who have understood this fact have been strong comrades in these moments of strike (particularly the core from 2008-2009 on Pond Road whose politicization has stuck), whereas those who did not take the struggle seriously drifted along as so many philosophers drift.

Seventhly, Devin Z. Shaw who not only blurbed this book but

has been a good out-of-city and ideologically adjacent comrade. Considering I bugged him for a blurb 2 years before I finally sent the manuscript of this book to publication he has been rather patient. In that time he helped organize a book launch in Ottawa for my 2017 *Austerity Apparatus*, where he asked me some excellent questions, and has supported my work in general. The fact that he succeeded in the holy grail of tenure in an era when tenure is disappearing speaks to the quality of his work, but it is also important to recognize he has refused to water down his anti-capitalist and combative politics. Just read *Continuity and Rupture* and think through the arguments, comrade, and you'll be in the Maoist camp within a year.

Thanks also to Matthew McLennan, Mateo Andante, and Cam McAlpine for their contributions. I first met Matt as part of the band, Consumer Goods, fronted by our friend Tyler Shipley back when we were all grad students and now I'm glad to know that another radical is teaching philosophy. Mateo Andante I met over Twitter as the politically committed "Mexican Philosopher" whose dedication to exposing the limits of bourgeois philosophy made him a perfect person to ask for an endorsement blurb. Cam's design skills are rivaled only by his political practice and I am very grateful that he helped fix the only diagram in this book, transforming it into an image that was much cleaner than the clunky version I had initially proposed.

Ninthly, I must recognize Christophe Kistler who has been bugging me for an acknowledgement since he republished and distributed *The Communist Necessity* in Europe. Really, he should have been named in the acknowledgements of *Methods Devour Themselves* because of his love (and his partner's love) of SFF. I've enjoyed the many conversations and arguments we have had over instant messaging and apologize that they became less frequent over the past few years. I hope you'll enjoy this work and look forward to engaging with your thoughts as we struggle together across continents...even though I'm a "noob". If you ever visit Toronto you have a place to stay.

Next, Benjanun Sriduangkaew deserves recognition mainly because I used one of her stories as an analogical device for this book. This is in fact the third time I've acknowledged Bee: the first was in *Austerity Apparatus* because she wrote a blurb for it, the second was in *Methods Devour Themselves* since that was a book we wrote together. To go all Hegelian for the moment, while this acknowledgement of Bee is temporally later than the previous acknowledgements, it remains conceptually prior since I had already conceptualized the prologue of this manuscript in reference to her *Comet's Call* story before she agreed to blurb *Austerity Apparatus* and before *Methods Devour Themselves* was put together. This book might have been published later, but it helped forge the relationship behind the previous two publications.

Second-to-last, my colleague and friend, Shyam Ranganathan, is someone who has affected this project in a subtle manner. Although Shyam's work concerns the "Eastern" philosophical tradition, and though this book necessarily deals with the mystified hegemony of the "Western canon", our various discussions and debates influenced the trajectory of *Demarcation and Demystification*. Whereas Shyam's project is concerned with centring non-Western philosophical trajectories, rejecting the peripheralizing Orientalist narrative that relegates them to the non-philosophical realm of religion or mysticism, my project here was in undermining the centrality of the philosophical conceit that resulted in the "Western canon" in the first place. I'm sure that Shyam will disagree with some of my universal claims about philosophy, but these are disagreements that, far from hostile, will lead to some great discussions when we are both able to navigate our parenting schedules and get together.

Finally, and as always, my life partner Vicky has to be acknowledged. There is not a single book that has not been written outside of her influence since all of my work reflects discussions we have had (and are still having) and is produced under the assumption that she is the main reader... "what will she think about this?" is thus the guiding thought of every sentence, paragraph, and chapter I construct. This is not to relegate her to the position of some abstract muse, which is entirely chauvinistic, because lord knows that she also curates shows, creates art, and writes essays with me in mind as a reader. We've been influencing each others' thought for a long time and the fact that we don't always agree simply means that we've been carrying on an exciting and engaging extended debate for years. This book, unlike some of the others, is one that she worked hard to edit before I sent it to submission. She found so many redundancies in the original draft that I was completely embarrassed. Moreover, the opening analogy that used Bee's story exists mainly because she told me, years ago, that I needed a "beautiful opening analogy" to motivate a book on philosophy. I'm happy to report that opening analogy received her full endorsement. It's good to have a Fine Arts intellectual as a spouse; it encourages you to make your non-fiction more engaging—like an installation. And, if I can just promote her for a moment, the installations Vicky has curated, and the ones she has made me see, have been invaluable.

CULTURE, SOCIETY & POLITICS

Contemporary culture has eliminated the concept and public figure of the intellectual. A cretinous anti-intellectualism presides, cheer-led by hacks in the pay of multinational corporations who reassure their bored readers that there is no need to rouse themselves from their stupor. Zer0 Books knows that another kind of discourse – intellectual without being academic, popular without being populist – is not only possible: it is already flourishing. Zer0 is convinced that in the unthinking, blandly consensual culture in which we live, critical and engaged theoretical reflection is more important than ever before.

If you have enjoyed this book, why not tell other readers by posting a review on your preferred book site.

Malign Velocities
Accelerationism and Capitalism
Benjamin Noys
Long listed for the Bread and Roses Prize 2015, *Malign Velocities* argues against the need for speed, tracking acceleration as the symptom of the ongoing crises of capitalism.
Paperback: 978-1-78279-300-7 ebook: 978-1-78279-299-4

Meat Market
Female Flesh under Capitalism
Laurie Penny
A feminist dissection of women's bodies as the fleshy fulcrum of capitalist cannibalism, whereby women are both consumers and consumed.
Paperback: 978-1-84694-521-2 ebook: 978-1-84694-782-7

Romeo and Juliet in Palestine
Teaching Under Occupation
Tom Sperlinger
Life in the West Bank, the nature of pedagogy and the role of a university under occupation.
Paperback: 978-1-78279-637-4 ebook: 978-1-78279-636-7

Sweetening the Pill
or How We Got Hooked on Hormonal Birth Control
Holly Grigg-Spall
Has contraception liberated or oppressed women? *Sweetening the Pill* breaks the silence on the dark side of hormonal contraception.
Paperback: 978-1-78099-607-3 ebook: 978-1-78099-608-0

Why Are We The Good Guys?
Reclaiming your Mind from the Delusions of Propaganda
David Cromwell
A provocative challenge to the standard ideology that Western
power is a benevolent force in the world.
Paperback: 978-1-78099-365-2 ebook: 978-1-78099-366-9

Readers of ebooks can buy or view any of these bestsellers by
clicking on the live link in the title. Most titles are published
in paperback and as an ebook. Paperbacks are available in
traditional bookshops. Both print and ebook formats are available
online.
Find more titles and sign up to our readers' newsletter
at http://www.johnhuntpublishing.com/culture-and-politics
Follow us on Facebook
at https://www.facebook.com/ZeroBooks
and Twitter at https://twitter.com/Zer0Books